Praise for *A Mindful Move*

"Kiran has written a thought-provoking, insightful, and warm book combining anecdotes, examples, and research in an engaging and accessible way. She provides a very useful resource for anyone thinking of moving or who has already gone through relocation, helping to unravel the complex layers of geographical and emotional transition and provide strategies for success. A welcome addition to any relocation toolkit!"

—Rachel Yates, founder of The Expat LifeLine and coauthor of *Finding Home Abroad: A Guided Journal for Adapting to Life Overseas*

"In our global society, change has become inevitable for many, but the emotional effects of change are rarely addressed. Finally, a book written for all of us who have moved from family, friends, and the comfortable familiarity of 'home.' Kiran Prasad gives helpful insight and useable guidance on how to overcome our feelings, feel a part of new surroundings, and make new best friends."

—Margaret Ferrell, relocation specialist

"Loss is a part of life, and grief is a natural consequence of loss. Kiran Prasad has given us another facet of grief to ponder—with the powerful tool of mindfulness and her one-of-a-kind implementation of it. What a support to others who didn't know why they felt the way they did."

—Georgena Eggleston, trauma specialist and author of *A New Mourning: Discovering the Gifts in Grief*

"*A Mindful Move* addresses a major life transition whose inner turmoil is endured by most persons several times throughout their lives, and whose nature was described by novelist D.H. Lawrence: disconnection from the familiar; the honeymoon with the new; homesickness for the old; and one's eventual connection with the new. This fourfold inner transition is thoroughly mapped in *A Mindful Move*, with a profound sensitivity that can significantly ease the distress of any reader who is either facing a change of homestead, is in the midst thereof, or who has yet to complete the creative pause of an earlier relocation."

—Rev. Noel McInnis, New Thought Center for Spiritual Living

A Mindful Move

Feel at Home Again

By Kiran Prasad

First Edition

ISBN-13: 978-0-9971672-0-7

ISBN-10: 0-9971672-0-3

Library of Congress Control Number: 2017900703
Sun Path Publishing, Lake Oswego, OR

Cover design by Liana Moisescu

Front cover image by Frenta/Bigstockphoto.com

Author photo by Pete Springer

"East or west, home is the best."

In loving memory of my mother.
I will always miss her warm, tight hugs,
sweet smile, and caring nature.

Contents

Foreword

As a young child, Kiran Prasad relocated from India to England in what would be the start of a lifetime of moving across continents and cultures. When our paths first crossed, she was writing *A Mindful Move* and coming to terms with many past moves, only to be faced with another possible geographical relocation that was largely out of her control. She began to ask questions of friends, family, mental health professionals, and spiritual teachers. Although her quest was not without its difficulties, its outcome is presented in this book, which is written with insight, wisdom, and compassion.

A Mindful Move includes great tips on what to do, what to avoid, and how to get through what for most of us is a life-changing event. Kiran addresses various emotional responses to the upheaval involved in relocation: joy, depression, anxiety, anger, and uncertainty about what home really is and what it means to each of us. As a psychologist, I appreciate her knack for educating readers in a way that makes the entire process accessible and understandable. She writes with empathy, sensitivity, and humor that will help anyone wrap their head and heart around a recent or upcoming relocation.

My favorite part of the book is Kiran's insight that home is not external, but internal. She believes that "internally, a feeling of home is when we feel at home with ourselves." She also examines the human need to belong, which is especially difficult when the relocation crosses cultural boundaries.

Readers of *A Mindful Move* will likely feel validated and supported as Kiran puts words around their experiences. There are also useful nuggets regarding loneliness, culture shock, loss of identity, and self-esteem. Readers inclined toward mindfulness and spirituality will be glad to see these concepts discussed in language they recognize, and readers who are new to these concepts will find valuable tips that they can apply to their daily lives.

Kiran's writing shows how much she has evolved during her journeys, from a young child moving to a foreign country to someone whose maturity has allowed her to reach out to people from all walks of life who are facing the challenge of relocation. This deeply philosophical and spiritual book helps us look inside ourselves, understand who we are, and make peace with life's adversities. Because if we're at peace with ourselves, we can feel at home anywhere.

William Robert Cavasher, Ph.D.

Dr. Cavasher is a licensed clinical psychologist in Portland, Oregon. He works with teens, families, and adults who need help with anxiety, depression, and relationships. He helped found the Returning Veterans Project and does pro bono work with veterans who suffer from PTSD. He also works with adults who were sexually abused as children.

Author's Note

Who this Book Is for

If you're relocating for the first time, struggling with a current move, or simply trying to learn more about the moving process, this book is for you. The people who'll gain the most from it are accompanying spouses or partners, especially if they have children. It's difficult to accept change if the decision wasn't yours.

What It's About

A Mindful Move is about how to transition from loss and sadness to acceptance after relocating to a new place. It includes ways to deal with grief, loneliness, and culture shock, and approaches to help children and pets adjust. A move involves unpacking more than your possessions; it's about unpacking your life and having to reassemble your identity.

This book will:

- Help you understand the psychological challenges of moving.
- Provide a well-defined process to guide you through your transition.
- Provide tools such as mindfulness practices to embrace being here now.

Why I Wrote It

The hardest part of moving comes after the packing and unpacking are over. I wrote this book to provide new-comers with the support I wish I received during that time. Generally, people help with physical things such as babysitting or cooking meals. There's also support from books and online materials with checklists for the big day. But there's little support for the emotional trauma that can follow.

Months after relocating, I had no one to turn to who understood my challenges, because once you've un-packed and set up your home, people expect all to be well. In Susan Miller's book *After the Boxes Are Unpacked*, I finally found someone I could relate to, and in Robin Pascoe's *A Moveable Marriage*, I found a wonderful reflec-tion of my own life as an accompanying spouse. These books were the catalysts that inspired me to write my own.

How My Perspective Changed

A Mindful Move was a long work in progress that evolved with me over many years. It seems that every time I got close to completing it, something prevented me. At times I was physically unable to write because of my health. Then further life transitions left me emotionally unable to finish it. What finally pulled me out of this slump was when I accepted my "new normal" and stopped wishing I could turn the clock back. Everything happens for a reason, and perhaps this book was delayed to allow me extra time to add more richness to it. This came in the form of spirituality. By that I don't mean religion, but positive psychology and tools for personal transformation.

How It Got Its Title

A Mindful Move wasn't what I originally intended to call this book—it was going to be *Neither Here Nor There*. I wasn't trying to find another title; it found me. It was after I joined a spiritual center and met and interviewed the delightful Reverend Kathleen McKern Verigin for the book, that the title arose.

One day, as I was listening to that recorded interview, I came across the word "mindful" in relation to moving. I'd been learning about mindfulness, and information about it kept appearing in various ways. Just the day before, I'd come across it three times. Was the universe trying to tell me something? All I know is, the words "a mindful move" popped into my head. I had a sudden realization, and something told me that I had to change the title, and my perspective on the book as a whole. Although it meant I would have to do further revisions that would delay publication, I went with it. It just felt right.

How It's Structured

My knowledge of relocation is based on my twenty-nine moves, the experiences of the thirty people I interviewed, and the opinions and research of experts in the field. I used what I learned to devise what I call the "the moving process." Part one of the book takes you through these stages and shows you how to progress through them.

Many of the tips I share are from my most difficult relocations as I was experiencing them. That's how I know they really work. Some of the challenges faced can be explained through Abraham Maslow's theory of human motivation. Therefore, I use it to structure part two of the book. Don't worry; I've explained it in simple terms, so you won't need a psychology degree to understand it! I also had a licensed therapist look over the psychological content to make sure I'm presenting it correctly.

I wish you the best in your new place and hope you feel at home again soon.

Kiran Prasad

Please note, I'm not a medical practitioner. Therefore, any suggestions must be taken at your own risk and are not meant to replace the advice of a healthcare professional. Also, I can't guarantee that what works for others will work for you, and I assume no responsibility for your actions. Some of the names of people interviewed for this book have been altered to protect their privacy.

Acknowledgments

I thank my sister Rita for being a great listener and best friend during my lonely times. I thank my brother Preet for providing material for this book, a reason to complete it quickly, and feedback and support. Thanks also to Elissa for welcoming me to America, to Stephanie, and later Roshini, for "adopting" me into their families, and to Donna for being the perfect neighbor and friend. To Olga, Denise, Laurie, Seema, and Anu for being supportive friends. To Natasha for introducing me to "the right kind of people" and Dorothy for coffee mornings and Robin Pascoe's books.

I owe my gratitude to Jani for rescuing me in my toughest week, and to other friends whose support sustained me. I also want to acknowledge all who shared their stories, especially Sanj for letting me shadow his move. A special acknowledgement goes to my college professors, Dr. Linda Pavonetti and Dr Ronald Cramer, for inspiring me to write for publication.

My deepest gratitude to my husband and children for allowing me to publish their experiences and providing the support to go ahead with this venture. In particular, Vinnie, for setting deadlines and both Nikita and Vinnie for helping revise and market my book.

Last, but not least, I thank my writing group (especially Tina, Leon, and Dan), my proofreaders Dan and Jonathan, as well as my professional editor.

I can't believe I did it! It wouldn't have been possible without you all.

Part One

The Process of Moving:

Understanding It All

Lost

It's 1:00am.
But all sense
Of time and place
Has deserted me
As I sit alone
Staring blankly
At the walls
Vaguely aware
Of the sounds of
A sleeping house
Lost
Trying to find
My way home

Kiran Prasad

Chapter 1

Understanding Loss

Anyone who has lost something they thought was theirs forever finally comes to realize that nothing really belongs to them.

PAULO COELHO

It was Monday morning, almost two months into my twenty-ninth move. After my husband and teenage children had left for the day, I went upstairs. Instead of getting ready to go out for a walk as I'd planned, I got back in bed and lay there thinking of the life I'd left behind and the people I missed. Tears rolled down my face. I thought, *I could just lie here all day. Who would care?* I had nowhere to go, no one to see, nothing in particular to do. A cloud swept over me, and the sounds of the world faded away.

After some time, I pushed myself to get up, literally using self-talk. I rushed into the shower and told myself, "Go, get dressed, and do something . . . anything! Don't let yourself sink into despair!" I started thinking of the song "Bridge over Troubled Water" and my eyes welled up again as I sang the words. Then I cried hysterically as if someone had died! It helped release all the emotion I'd been keeping inside, a catharsis that led to a turning point in my move.

I finally went out for a walk as I'd originally intended, and felt somewhat better for it. The mango-golden leaves of Oregon had fallen across my path up the hill and they got me thinking about change, all the transitions a person goes through in life and how we somehow get through them. It made me think of my sister losing her husband to cancer. It takes time for the pain to ease. Whatever the cause of a major change in a person's life, the process of healing from it is basically the same. There's a grieving period for what was lost and eventually an acceptance that things will never be the same again.

After an invigorating walk, I came back inside and typed what would become the first pages of *A Mindful Move*. Throughout the rest of this book, I'll share the strategies I used—and those used by others—to shift out of sadness and loss into a place of acceptance.

One of the best strategies I know is to be mindful. What I mean by that is to be in the present moment. The idea of mindfulness isn't new; it's been around for a while through Buddhist philosophies and practices. But it was Dr. Jon Kabat-Zinn, a scientist, writer, and meditation teacher, who brought it to the medical community and showed how it could be used to reduce anxiety and stress. He describes mindfulness as focusing on the here and now, being fully present in whatever you do and wherever you are. When thoughts begin to wander to the future or past, that's okay. Just avoid judgment and let them glide out of your mind like clouds. Practicing mindfulness meditation can help us improve at doing this.

The present moment is where life happens, yet we give it little space in our minds. Relocation coach Maripat Abbott explains on her blog that "most of us struggle with living in the present moment. Thoughts of the future or the past tend to occupy more of our mind than they should. If this is a common dynamic in regular activities, can you imagine what it is like during relocation? When you are moving from one city to another and one home to another, you are often holding two separate locations in your mind at the same time; you are not fully present in either one."

Being mindful during this time is easier said than done. Even though I've relocated a lot and know how to transition well, sometimes I still find my thoughts straying to the past. This is because no one is immune to the heartache of grief. In Sarah Kershaw's *New York Times* article "The Psychology of Moving," psychoanalyst Ronnie Greenberg points out that "moving is incredibly stressful and people don't realize it—they mainly talk about the packing and external part of moving." But change affects us internally, too.

Transition and Change

The words "transition" and "change" are often confused with each other, when really they're quite different. Change happens externally when we experience a new situation, whereas transition happens internally—it's the emotional shift needed to adjust to that situation. It isn't easy to make that shift because transition involves uncertainty, and the unknown causes fear. I've got an ornamental rock that's engraved with the saying "Nothing in life is certain but uncertainty." These words are etched onto my heart now because I've faced so many changes and the pain that came with them.

How we respond to change

Not everyone responds to change the way I do. Our circumstances affect how we respond. When it comes to relocation, this can include our age, health, support systems, reason for moving, losses and gains, and the people accompanying us. Our personality affects our response as well. Some of us are naturally more spontaneous or ad-venturous and get itchy feet, while others prefer stability and familiar surroundings. Lisa and her husband Mark, two Brits living in America, admit that they both have wanderlust. As I interviewed them for this book, they were already planning their next move. Five years in one spot is too long for them. They prefer to switch locations every two years, and they enjoy the excitement of it all.

Personally, I need stability and familiar surroundings. But by the time I started writing this book, I'd relocated one too many times and was burnt out from having to continuously readjust. When my health began to deteriorate because of my moves to the point of disability, I struggled to feel at home again. I'll share more about this in later chapters.

It wasn't easy overcoming the challenges of a migratory life, but now I'm able to appreciate how it made me into a stronger, more resilient woman. Change can cause loss and heartache, but it can also bring the opportunity for growth. To embrace the new, we're often required to let go of the old.

Facing Loss

Cumulative losses

Whether we relocate because of an unexpected life change or a choice, it's never easy to face the series of losses that follow. In my shift from Indiana to Oregon, I left behind a beautiful home, a wonderful job and the sense of identity I'd built around it, supportive friends, a safe and tight-knit community, and, eventually, my health. On top of it all, we lost financially on the sale of our house and the contents we couldn't take with us. Then, when we discovered that a few of our belongings had been damaged during delivery, I could take it no more. I was surprised by my overreaction.

Maybe there's a saturation point for loss, and once it's reached, even the slightest additional loss is too much to bear. Bob Deits, the author of *Life After Loss*, observes that "whatever loss you experienced caused you to have a series of losses. Each one hits at the core of how you measure your happiness and the value of your life . . . even so-called 'minor' losses can have a far-reaching impact on your life."

My friend Debbie faced cumulative loss when her husband was offered a job in upper management. They relocated from one part of Michigan to another, and at first she felt the loss of the usual things, such as her house, friends, and neighbors. But within a month of getting there (and after they'd bought an expensive, larger house), her husband lost his job, followed by his health. She became ill, too, and for a while the doctors didn't know what was wrong with her. Four months later, she found out she was pregnant! It was the last thing they needed right then. Her husband didn't know what to do, and many things went wrong from there.

Debbie's usually a positive woman who can turn a challenging move around for herself, but with this one, she couldn't. It was one loss too many, and it became overwhelming. In fact, until I interviewed her, she says that she'd completely blocked this move from her memory!

The loss and gain equation

The number of losses we experience can affect our ability to recover from them. I call this the "loss and gain equation" of moving. We're less able to accept the sacrifices and hardships that relocation brings if we lose more than we gain. Transition expert William Bridges' groundbreaking book *Transitions: Making Sense of Life's Changes* explains how a transition is "endurable if it means something—if it is part of a movement toward a desired end. But if it is not related to some larger and beneficial pattern, it becomes simply distressing."

My husband initiated most of my moves after marriage, and they created greater losses than gains for me. I reluctantly agreed to relocate our family to support him in his climb up the career ladder. While he was upward-bound, I felt like a game piece on a Chutes and Ladders board, climbing up the ladder by the end of one move, only to come down the chute on the next, never really getting anywhere. I simply went through the motions without a sense of control. For a long time, I had no real understanding of how loss affects us, until I learned about grief.

Grieving the Losses

Based on the work of Elisabeth Kübler-Ross, the five stages of grief are denial, anger, bargaining, depression, and, finally, acceptance. Although they are described as stages, they don't have to happen in this order, and not everyone goes through all of them. Grief is personal. However, I believe that healing from relocation grief can be accelerated and made less painful by taking a structured approach and staying mindful through it.

First, we have to acknowledge losses by allowing ourselves to mourn them. By accepting our feelings, we're better able to deal with them and get on with our lives. Dana, who has two children and lives in Michigan, admits that she was in denial after her house caught fire. She still threw a planned outdoor party for forty kids just ten minutes after the fire was put out and the firemen left.

Another type of denial is when we put something we've lost on a pedestal and only see the rosy side of it. We might do that with our previous home, neighborhood, or friends. After losing something dear, there's a tendency to remember only the good, or even to make it out to be better than it was.

Sometimes we try to fill the void that a loss creates by finding something similar to replace it. Perhaps we decorate our house in the same style as before, make friends who remind us of previous ones, or search for similar stores to shop at. Nothing can replace what was lost, and wishing it would magically return only keeps us from getting on with our life. At some point, it's necessary to let go of the past, accept our reality, and find a way forward. The moving process—and staying mindful through it—can help.

The Moving Process

Although we all respond to loss differently, we go through a common process when we relocate. Based on the stages of grief, as well as transition and culture shock (which I'll explain later), I've devised what I call "the moving process." I hope it will help you understand the emotions you're going through and make it easier to work through them.

The moving process is made up of the following phases: disconnection, honeymoon, homesickness, and connection.

The disconnection phase

Disconnection, the first phase, is about physical and emotional preparation. Just as we disconnect our houses from utility services such as water and electricity when we prepare to relocate, so do we disconnect from people, places, and things. This process involves accepting the fact that we're leaving, and saying goodbye to those parts of our life. While we might reconnect later, we have to loosen the ties in order to depart. Relinquishing them isn't easy, and feelings of grief such as anger, guilt, or sadness can begin at this point.

The honeymoon phase

This phase starts in the first weeks after arriving in a new place, and usually lasts only a short while. It's when reality hasn't sunk in yet and everything feels fresh and exciting, like a vacation. It's also a time for bridging the old life with the new. Depending on the circumstances, this phase might be skipped altogether.

The homesickness phase

This is the most challenging period, and it often begins a month or so after arrival and can last up to a year or more. It's when the reality hits and we become homesick. It might show up as inertia, even depression. In the early part of this phase, there's a tendency to want to run back to where we came from. We can get stuck in a rut and feel like we're neither here nor there.

The connection phase

Connection is the last phase of the moving process, and the end goal. A sense of connection, or of feeling at home, can start at any time, although studies show that it usually happens after a year. It occurs when we transition through homesickness and become a local resident again, involved and connected. For this to happen, unmet needs have to be addressed.

The stages of moving are not necessarily linear, which means we can go back and forth between them at our own pace. The goal, however, is to come to accept living in our new location. We'll take a closer look at these phases in the next chapters, starting with disconnection, or what we have to do to leave well.

Rooted Here

How I long to be
Like an old oak tree
With its anchoring
Roots
Standing still
In the very place
Where it first began
In its green familiarity
Community
How I long
To be rooted here.

Kiran Prasad

Chapter 2

Leaving Well

What we call the beginning is often the end. And to make an end is to make a beginning. The end is where we start from.

T.S. ELIOT

When we lived in Michigan, my son Vinnie was a teenager, and my daughter Nikita was a pre-teen. When they found out that we might be moving again, they took out their frustrations on me. I was equally angry at the news, because we were settled after living in the same city (on and off) for eleven years. The children were well established in their school and friend circles, and I was happy as a teacher and busy mom. I'd also invested time and energy into making our house a home. None of us wanted to leave. We protested! In the end, though, we had no choice but to resign ourselves to being uprooted again. Our anger somewhat dissipated as we got busy preparing to leave.

Although we were busy, we made time to say goodbye to close friends such as the Pacione family. We met with them at our favorite ice cream parlor. When it was time to leave, our children took one last photo together, and my friend Lorna hugged me tightly and cried. I'll never forget it; she cried as though we'd never meet again. I felt guilty because I didn't share her sadness yet. Instead, I kept telling her I wasn't going far, and that we'd stay in touch. I was in denial, and I behaved as if we were relocating to the next town instead of the next state.

The disconnection phase is the first part of the moving process, and it begins the moment we know we're leaving. It's about letting go and taking steps to disengage from our current life and prepare for the next. Connections to people, places, and things have to be loosened, at least temporarily.

William Bridges explains that endings are the starting points of transitions. They're part of his Transition Model, which he describes in *Managing Transitions*. The first step of his model is Endings: letting go of the old. Next is the Neutral Zone, where we explore the new in order to become comfortable with it. The last step is Beginnings, when we're finally able to embrace what we couldn't before.

During this time of "endings," we can experience feelings of grief: shock, denial, numbness, fear, and anger. It's important to acknowledge all of them and accept the fact that we're moving.

Acknowledging the Move

Discuss with those involved

One way to acknowledge a move is to discuss it with those involved to prepare them. Discussion is healthy: it allows us to share feelings as well as to ask questions and can prevent us from carrying emotional baggage. We all need plenty of time to process everything.

However, with young children it might be best to tell them closer to the move date. It's also important to stay positive in front of children, because they tend to mirror their parents, especially the primary caregiver. Sarah, from Oregon, says that when she was six, she couldn't believe she was moving. "I just giggled at the name

'Bangladesh' and at how intense Mom and Dad sounded. Although I was confused and mostly sad about leaving my best friend, it was okay because my parents were enthusiastic, and their word was still gospel."

Teenagers, on the other hand, are more likely to resent being uprooted. When they're included in decision-making, however, it helps them process emotions and maintain a sense of control. Sarah explains how her response to having her world overturned was different when she was sixteen: "I was moving to Nairobi, and I threw a massive fit. I couldn't cope. I fought with my parents every day. I complained and whined to my friends . . . I was a demon child!" Not everyone is able to express emotions this easily. Watch out for children who wear a veil of excitement, when underneath it they're anxious.

After discussing with family, let other loved ones know; they, too, need to get used to the idea that you're leaving. Wait until everything is confirmed, however. My family has experienced the awkwardness of telling everyone we're relocating but then having a change of plans. My daughter's preschool even threw her a farewell party, only to find out shortly after that we weren't moving! (That was an embarrassing conversation, to say the least.)

If you've been through this too, you're not alone. It happens a lot, especially to expats who are transferred frequently. It can disrupt relationships, since people naturally disengage from someone who's leaving.

Loosen the cord to your relationships

Once you know for sure that you're relocating, loosen the cord to your relationships. Get used to spending less time with those you're moving away from—it can prepare you for seeing them rarely or not at all. This is only general advice, however; every situation is different, and you might prefer to spend quality time with loved ones while you still can.

Loosen the ties to your home

Depersonalize your space

Another way to acknowledge a move is to loosen the ties to your home. When we were ready to put our house on the market, we'd depersonalize the space, putting away all personal items such as photos, certificates, and trophies. We'd take down items that affiliated us with anything or revealed our identities, including religious, cultural, political, and sporting items. It was a way of creating a neutral environment that allowed potential buyers to walk through and imagine living in the house.

A few times, this endeavor included toning down vibrant paint colors and unique décor. Not everyone can relate to a bedroom with a princess or a space theme! My dad had painstakingly helped me decorate most of the houses we lived in. I still remember how long it took us to figure out how to paint clouds on the ceiling and castles on the walls of the children's rooms! In the end, as heartbreaking as it was, we had to cover up my dad's artistry with neutral colors. Home-staging professionals consider depersonalizing to be one of their most important strategies. It makes a house visually appealing to anyone.

Throughout our moves, we depersonalized so many times that my children became experts at it. We'd have fun pretending to be prospective buyers and making sure we'd left no trace of our identities. Weeks before my son,

Vinnie, was getting ready to leave for college, I got him to depersonalize his room. He removed his posters and other personal items and packed them to take to his college dorm. It mentally prepared him for leaving.

Another thing that always prepared my mind was the "For Sale" sign in the front yard. I know it's not always possible to put up a sign, but if you can, it will help you accept that you're leaving.

Preparing Well

As we get ready to close one chapter of our life and transition to the next, we can become overwhelmed by everything we have to do. This is when good planning comes in. By anticipating change and preparing for it, we can reduce anxiety about the unknown and regain control.

When preparing to move, it's important to understand your unique needs—everyone's situation is different. Nikki Phipps, an author on familylobby.com, writes about blended families and their special challenges. She explains how family members don't fit together perfectly like *The Brady Bunch*. They have family histories, traditions, memories, and sometimes even different cultures to take into account.

My friend Janika, a single mom, went through those challenges. It's not surprising that she was nervous before moving in with her boyfriend, his children, and his mother. It was a huge decision to blend households, especially since she hadn't lived with anyone for a while. For so long, she'd been used to being single, doing things her way, and keeping things where she wanted. She had to mentally prepare for losing privacy and space, with kids and pets from both families merging into one household. She admits that she didn't really prepare her boyfriend and his family for all this. It was pretty crazy at first, especially since she relocated during Christmas!

On the other hand, Mark and his wife Lisa, who have moved often, prepare meticulously. They understand only too well how it will impact them. Mark explained that because the cost and logistics of transferring from England to America were horrendous, they developed a system. They made a checklist of all the things they had to do, based on what they learned from previous moves. It was a process they started months ahead. Mark, a project manager by profession, says he treated it like any other work assignment and applied those skills to it.

We can't all be project managers, but we can make a list of what needs to be done, create deadlines for each task, assign responsibilities, and decide which items require urgent attention. Tasks can be broken into manageable chunks to work on each day. As a homemaker, I focused on things related to my children and home. Whatever your focus, a pre-visit to the location you're thinking about moving to is vital.

Arrange a pre-visit

Involve kids

A pre-visit has many benefits, including acclimating you to the environment. If you have children, I suggest taking them with you as long as they're old enough to benefit from it. Include them in finding a house and schools, and know in advance when schools close for the year. For us, in Oregon, it was May, which meant a summer move would be best. We would relocate then because it would give our children more time to settle in before school started. As a teacher, I know that it's easier for children to adjust if they start the academic year with everyone else, and this timing is especially important for shy kids. To smooth their transition, then, our pre-visit was done in the spring.

A summer move has its drawbacks too, however. In America, it means that incoming students have lonely months ahead while other children are away at camp or on vacation. When we relocated to Oregon, my son Vinnie was sixteen and my daughter Nikita was fourteen. We registered them for activities as soon as possible. The high school was kind enough to let my daughter try out for a team during our pre-visit, which meant that she could begin training in the summer and make friends before school started. We also picked up a school directory to figure out where most students lived. Then we looked for houses in those neighborhoods. Living close to other school families meant we could carpool, and our children could make friends easily.

Anne, a therapist by profession, understands the importance of preparing well and helping family members adjust quickly. This is why she drove her son across the country to a school-orientation day before they relocated. She wanted him to experience what it would be like walking through those corridors, because he was going from a school of a hundred kids to one of six hundred. In addition to that, she arranged for him to check out the local Boy Scouts troop, which would provide an important social outlet in addition to its other benefits. As a family, they tried out various churches to find the best fit, treating their comfort with the congregation as an important consideration before making this huge transition.

Other benefits of a pre-visit

A pre-visit has other benefits too, depending on your situation. If you're still job-hunting, it's an opportunity to collect application forms or set up meetings with prospective employers. It's also an ideal time to pick up a driving manual and registration forms if you have to take a test.

Get rid of physical clutter

Benefits of decluttering

After visiting the location and finding a house or apartment, it's easier to figure out how much stuff to cut back on. And cutting down on clutter has additional benefits: researchers at the Princeton University Neuroscience Institute found that reducing clutter helps us think more clearly. Their study, published in the January 2011 issue of *The Journal of Neuroscience*, concludes that we are less irritable, more productive, less distracted, and better able to process information if we have an uncluttered house and office.

Lisa, our frequent mover, adds that getting rid of unwanted items also decreases costs, leaves us with less to pack and unpack, and feels liberating. But how exactly do we go about it?

Ways to cut back on clutter

Lisa suggests that if we want to keep a few sentimental items, we should restrict them to a small box. Another option I recommend is to photograph them for remembrance. I did this with several art projects that my little Rembrandts created in preschool!

Before leaving to volunteer with the Peace Corps in Macedonia, Amaya, who's a teacher, found a creative way to recycle her unwanted items. She threw a party for herself and her students and made them customized buckets full of things she didn't need anymore.

Don't underestimate how long it takes to declutter. It's not until we start packing that we realize how much we've accumulated. We can start with one room, closet, drawer, or category (such as books) at a time. Even fifteen minutes a day makes a difference. We can reduce clutter by returning borrowed items, taking things to consignment stores, advertising in newspapers and online, or giving things away.

I tried garage sales a couple of times, but found it wasn't worth the effort. I didn't even make as much money as I would have gotten back as a tax deduction if I'd donated everything! My friend Lee, a certified public accountant (CPA), agrees that donating makes more financial sense. He informs me that The Salvation Army even has a valuation guide for donations.

If you're going to give to a charity, be aware of when their busiest times are. In my part of the world, it's summer. Charities that do pickups can get fully booked out then, as we discovered! Also, know that some of them charge a small fee to cover for gas.

If you're using a company to transport belongings, be aware that there are things they won't pack onto the truck. Get this list early to allow time to decide what to do with these items, which include flammable, toxic, or hazardous materials such as alcohol, candles, batteries, and fire extinguishers. They won't transport valuables either, such as cash, checks, or expensive jewelry.

Things to buy

If family members or pets have dietary or medical needs, it's a good idea to stock up on those items. Also, decide whether to buy anything that will not be readily available or affordable in your next location.

Farewell gifts

As for gifts: I hate accumulating stuff and discourage friends from giving us farewell gifts. I do appreciate meaningful or practical ones, however. If you're lucky enough to be asked what type of gift you'd want, ask for something that takes little to no packing space. You could ask for a gift certificate for a massage, a book about your destination, or photos of friends.

Prepare medically

Moving can affect our health, as it did with Anne, who has fibromyalgia, a chronic pain and fatigue condition. Anne is also a caregiver to her husband, who's chronically ill. She had to postpone her relocation by several days because after she sat down to pack, she couldn't get off the floor. It's not surprising that she prepares medically for each family member, especially after that experience. Before relocating, she finds out where to get different types of medical care. You can't leave anything to chance as far as health is concerned!

I recommend getting a physical exam, including dental and vision, before leaving. Physicals are usually required for schools and jobs anyway, and if you already know which school your children will attend, you can download or request physical-exam or sports-clearance forms in advance. When you go for doctor appointments, save yourself another trip by filling out the medical consent form to allow records to be taken with you. Another option is to have your health records transmitted to future doctors. (This beats packing them and paying photocopying fees.)

Before we depart, I make sure everyone gets a haircut as well—it's easier to do these things on familiar ground. I have painful memories of having my thick, long hair butchered by stylists who weren't used to it.

Prepare your pets

Pets should also have a physical exam and any necessary vaccination boosters before leaving. (This is essential when an animal is being boarded.) If you're relocating your pet via air or with a moving company by road, this needs to happen a number of days before the trip (ten days in our case). You usually have to include this information on a travel certificate for animals being transported.

If your pet has a microchip, remember to update the electronic information it contains as well. We should have those for toddlers too! Finally, remember to get a new identification tag for your pet's collar as soon as you know your address and phone number. I found it safer to put my cell number on it. When we arrived at our house in Oregon, our dog nearly escaped from the yard while still wearing his old ID tag. Like us, he was keen to explore the territory!

A note for moving day: Watch your pets and kids!

For our transfer to America, we used a professional company, and I asked them about the most interesting thing they'd ever packed. One of the men replied that pets have a habit of crawling inside boxes or furniture, and he'd once ended up packing a cat! Luckily, it was discovered in time. I can imagine toddlers wanting to do the same! If you can, try to have someone look after pets and small children on moving day.

Before setting off for your new destination, another thing you can do to prepare for a successful transition is to learn about the local area—this will set realistic expectations and avoid misunderstandings.

Learn about the local area

You can find out how safe a location is and which areas to avoid by going online and visiting local news, radio, police websites, and social media pages. In America, city-data.com is particularly useful for comparing crime rates and types of crime. To get a sense of the demographics of a city, go to meetup.com and browse through the types of groups that meet there.

When Laura, a mother of two, returned to America from Singapore after her divorce, she thoroughly researched her local area. She found out about the usual things, plus information about local scams to avoid and requirements for establishing residency at the local, state, and country levels. It's important to learn not only about the local area, but about the culture you'll face, too.

Learn about the culture

There are various ways to tune in to a culture. You can connect with people who live or have lived there by using forums like citydata.com, social networking sites, conversations on the phone, or meetings over coffee. Jazz, who relocated from India to Canada for college, tells me that he talked to high school friends who'd already moved to Toronto to attend the same college.

When my son Vinnie was getting ready to go to college, he went to an alumni party in our area. He learned a lot by talking to the students, and he got to know other freshmen. Through Facebook, he stayed in touch with these students and he joined a Facebook group specifically for his dorm. Before he even attended his first class, he'd already started developing school spirit and identifying as a student there. He wore his college colors while still in high school and watched their games on television. All these things helped him connect to the culture.

Cultures vary as to how liberal or conservative they are. Gary, a young man we know, experienced this characteristic when he relocated internationally across England, Namibia, and Korea. Gary is originally from a liberal part of America, and after finally coming out as a gay man, he had to conceal that side of himself again when he lived abroad. Some of the cultures he was exposed to were extremely conservative and actively shunned—even physically hurt—gay people. He found that one of the hardest things is to have to re-navigate your identity and hide who you truly are. Understandably, he became quite paranoid about people discovering his secret and what that would mean for him. In one country, someone did find out: it was his boss at work, and Gary faced sexual harassment because of it.

Gary's advice to others planning to relocate is to ask locals what the perceptions are toward minorities. He recommends finding someone with similar values through a school or work network, as they would more likely give an honest opinion.

Learn the language

If you're relocating to a country where a foreign language is spoken, try to learn a little before getting there. Basic skills on arrival make everyday life a lot easier. Sarah, who previously lived in Bangladesh and Nairobi, says she didn't make any friends in her first year at a French-language school because she didn't speak French yet. She spent that year being completely miserable; it was so bad that she's blocked much of it from her memory.

As for me, when I moved to India at age eight, my parents hired a tutor to give my sisters and me a crash course in two Indian languages. I only wish we'd been taught these sooner, because we were under a lot of pressure from teachers to learn them very quickly. Years later, when my husband's job was being transferred to Germany, my children and I got a head start by listening to the language in the car. This time we jumped in too quickly, however, because that transfer didn't go through. At least my children learned a few words of German out of it. Hopefully when you leave for a foreign country you'll be equipped with basic phrases.

Gaining Closure

When it's finally time to leave your home, it can be hard to accept that you're going. Unlike a funeral that marks the end of a life, a move involves no memorial to mark the losses caused by relocation. Instead, we must find our own way of gaining closure.

In their landmark book *Third Culture Kids*, Ruth and David Pollock have a whole chapter on leaving one place and entering another because the experience is so significant. Using the clever acronym RAFT, they describe the four logs that are needed to build the raft that will carry us through a transition. These "logs" are Reconciliation, Affirmation, Farewell, and Think Destination.

Reconciliation is about resolving any conflicts you had with anyone in order to leave in peace. Affirmation is showing those you're leaving how much you love and/or appreciate them. Farewell is finding an honorable way to say goodbye. Finally, Think Destination is about being aware of how far you're moving from one another and valuing that last bit of quality time.

Farewell rituals

Many cultures have rites of passage or rituals to mark the end of one part of life and the start of another. They're comforting when everything around us is changing, and they allow us to express our grief.

Reverend Kathleen McKern Verigin, who focuses on creating rituals and ceremonies to transform lives, explained to me how rituals bridge the divide between our inner and outer worlds. When we relocate, she said, we have a really big outer-world change, so we need to create something to bridge it. She works with people to provide them with this link by showing them how to say goodbye to one house and hello to another.

She got the idea of using rituals to help with life changes when her father died. After the funeral in Iowa, Kathleen returned home while her mother started clearing out her father's things. Kathleen remembers wishing that she could've been there with her mother throughout that process. (She was camping at the time.) That's when she realized she could be there after all, by imagining her childhood home and mentally going into each room and letting memories surface. She visualized how the cookbooks used to be here or how they used to eat there. Finally, fourteen years after moving out of that house, Kathleen was able to say goodbye to each of those rooms.

Say goodbye

One important ritual that my family has for gaining closure is a farewell party. When I was leaving Indiana, a friend organized a huge potluck party for us at a park. This suited all ages of children and was a fun way to say goodbye. If you'd like a farewell party and no one organizes one for you, don't have a pity party and pout—throw one yourself! It doesn't have to be extravagant; it can be a simple celebration of your life in your old home and a time to share stories of happy times and talk about what you'll miss.

Revisiting favorite spots and taking pictures can also help bring closure to leaving your community, as can eating at a favorite restaurant or walking in the local park. These types of activities mark the last time you're a resident there.

However, you can only disconnect from something if you were connected to it in the first place. Katherine, who relocated from her childhood home to California with her boyfriend, says she hated the home she grew up in. It didn't represent anything happy for her or her family. She was glad to leave it and couldn't have run any faster from it. She didn't really say goodbye; she just took a leap.

Jenny, a widow who's retired, admits that she didn't really want to do anything to say goodbye when she was leaving. But her son encouraged her to. One thing she did was to give special cards to significant people, each with a saying on it that applied to them. Writer and publisher Jo Parfitt says farewell by writing lots of poetry. Jo has gone through many international moves and has lived in France, Dubai, Oman, the Netherlands, her native England, and Malaysia, where she currently resides. She tells me that she writes mostly sad poetry about not wanting to leave, and she published some of it in a book called *A Moving Landscape.*

As you can see, there's no right or wrong way to say goodbye, but it's important to mark your exit somehow. If you don't acknowledge an ending, it can stop you from transitioning forward. This happened to Debbie, who described how her relocation went so badly that later on she completely blocked it from her memory. She didn't prepare for the move to Canton, Michigan and didn't say goodbye to the place she left, largely because they were only a short distance from their previous home and she kept driving back there for various reasons. She admits she never really left, she just switched houses, yet it was too far away to keep up with her former life. She advises that we really have to let go and make a new life wherever we are.

Disengage from old roles

Not only do we have to say goodbye to people, places, and things, we also have to disconnect from other aspects of life there. Our work activities and projects—as well as various roles —have to come to an end.

It isn't easy to disengage from something that defined us for so long, even if we disliked it. I believe this is why we hang on to unsatisfactory jobs and relationships. Endings involve breaking habits and routines, and letting go. That's difficult for most of us. In the words of Reverend David Tinney, in a sermon given in 2008 at the First United Methodist Church in Vancouver, Washington, "If we want to move on, if we want new life to begin, if we want new growth to take root, we need to clear the soil of what is old."

Emotionally charged items

When a relationship breaks up, people try to clear the soil of what's old by returning personal items like gifts to free themselves of reminders of the past. Unfortunately, when we relocate, this is more complex because too many of our beloved possessions hold memories. Even the music we listen to regularly can make us sad and nostalgic, as it did for me. This makes it difficult to decide what to take and what to leave behind.

Do we want to start with fresh décor and furnishings or keep things the same? It depends on the association something has for us. Linda Binns, a self-described "breakthrough-energy expert" and feng shui specialist, tells me that "if you want to adjust to your new location as quickly as possible, release whatever you don't need, use, or love. Holding on to things just because of ties to another place can make the transition more difficult and keep you stuck in the past. Let go of anything that has negative associations—that's true whether you're moving or not."

I agree that while it's comforting to hold on to things that nurture us, it's best to let go of anything that prevents us from stepping forward and being in the present moment.

In the first months, I usually keep things the same, especially for children and pets. Transition experts agree that the first six months are the most difficult. For this reason, it's best to keeps things stable for a while. It's comforting to see something familiar when everything else has changed.

Clear emotional clutter

Finally, don't leave town without getting rid of emotional clutter. By this I mean forgive people who've upset you, apologize to those you've offended, and thank those who have done a lot for you. You might never get the chance again; I know this from bitter experience! Don't carry emotional baggage with you. It's unhealthy to hang on to the past.

My daughter, Nikita, always loved the idea of a clean slate, of leaving the mistakes of the past behind. As a teenager, she liked starting fresh. It's healthy to see endings in this way, as a "transition to another mode of being, a trial indispensible of regeneration; that is, to the beginning of a new life" as William Bridges describes in *Making Sense of Life's Changes*.

Maureen, who's moved often because of her husband's military career, admits that she doesn't believe we really get over the transitions we've been through in life. She certainly can't. Anyone who's lost a loved one knows that there are no neat endings when we face a major loss.

As you move forward, don't be surprised if you keep switching between disconnection and reconnection with your previous life. It's a normal reaction to grief. If you find yourself doing this, don't worry: chapter 4 includes strategies for dealing with homesickness, and the following chapter will also help. Just as it's important to leave a place well, it's vital to arrive well.

Where I'm From

I'm from the pink city of India
And the gray city of London.
I'm from colorful Punjabi suits
And dresses that my mother sewed.
I'm from freshly cooked chapattis
And from cream soda and fish and chips
(wrapped in newspaper).

I'm from children chasing
Ice cream vans
And milk delivered to the door.
Drinking milk in school
From small glass bottles.

I'm from "blackouts," paraffin lamps
And Bingo games.
I'm from English seasides
Where the shops sell
Candy floss and seaside rock
And shiny windmills on a stick.
I'm from picnics on a breezy beach
And beach balls blowing out to sea.

I'm from "health is wealth"
And the importance of calcium
And multivitamins
Vicks VapoRub for colds
A head massage
And chicken noodle soup.

I'm from a loving family
Who has taught me
The value of family.
Now, I have my own.

Kiran Prasad (credits to George Ella Lyon)

Chapter 3

Arriving Well

Savor the adventure and enjoy the taste of new cheese!
SPENCER JOHNSON

"Idyllic, like a resort area in Switzerland or a honeymoon destination" is how Rani, a realtor friend of mine, described Oregon when she first arrived here in the summer. She could've sold the place to anyone! There were vegetables she'd never seen, farmers' markets, and the beauty of rivers, streams, beaches, and flowers blooming. She was in love with Portland, the City of Roses, with its quaint cafes, pursuit of art, healthy food, casual lifestyle, and friendly people.

In these early honeymoon days, everything feels great, and as Robin Pascoe writes in *Raising Global Nomads*, "The similarities between cultures are often more obvious than the differences." We get an adrenaline rush from exploring fresh surroundings, doing different things, and meeting new people—much like a tourist does on an extended vacation.

However, excitement isn't the only feeling we experience at this time. Jazz had mixed emotions after he moved from India to Canada for college. He admitted to feeling anxious; Toronto was a foreign city with lots to explore—like Niagara Falls nearby, which he visited in the first couple of months. He found it daunting, yet exciting.

While the newness of everything is refreshing, it isn't relaxing, as a real vacation would be. There's much physical work to be done, with a to-do list that keeps growing. When Laura relocated from Singapore back to America after her divorce, she was frustrated. Although she was looking forward to getting settled in, she wanted to go out and explore instead of being stuck at home preparing for interviews and waiting around for repairmen and delivery men.

Smelling the Roses

If you're overwhelmed by the number of things you have to do, pause for a moment. Make time to smell the roses and really *be* there. If you think you're too busy to be mindful, the opposite's true. As Eckhart Tolle writes in his book *Stillness Speaks,* "To have your attention in the Now is not a denial of what is needed in your life. It is recognizing what is primary. Then you can deal with what is secondary with ease." He adds, "When your attention moves into the Now, there is an alertness. It is as if you were waking up from a dream, the dream of thought, the dream of past and future."

Being in the present moment helps us have a clearer mind to make decisions. It also allows us to better savor our new experiences.

Honeymoons Vary

How we feel during this phase depends on factors like our personality, circumstances, and expectations. For Rani, the place was as she expected because she'd done her research and prepared well. The natural charm and beauty of Oregon was exactly as people had described it.

Moreover, she knew what to expect in terms of the climate, which put her in a good frame of mind from the start.

No honeymoon

Amaya had a very different experience when she moved from New York City to Oregon. She didn't experience a honeymoon at all, probably because she was too busy trying to find a job and get her life back together again, and had little money to spend. She couldn't enjoy being in the new area, eating at interesting restaurants, or visiting exciting places. She also thinks she didn't experience a honeymoon period because the small town she relocated to didn't meet her expectations or represent who she is as a person.

Sunaina, a young lady who got married and moved to England to join her spouse, didn't experience this period either. She agrees with me that perhaps it's because there were already enough exciting things happening to her, including an actual honeymoon to an exotic location. It was also because, at first, the people and culture of her host country didn't quite live up to her expectations.

Anne, who has fibromyalgia, says her illness and the stress of having to do everything on her own prevented her from experiencing the honeymoon period. She had help with the packing, but at the other end, there was no one to assist her. If she could have afforded it, she would have hired someone to do it for her, and she probably would've had a better experience. Next time, she intends to do that, and says it's well worth putting aside money for. Her fibromyalgia flared up at times and she cried a lot because of the physical pain. On top of it all, she felt abandoned. She'd arrived expecting her friend since childhood to be there for her as a constant companion. She realizes now that she was being unrealistic.

Extended honeymoon

For frequent movers Mark and Lisa, on the other hand, the honeymoon lasts for ages. They can remain enamored with a place and feel like they're on an extended vacation for about two years—which is about how long they usually stay in a house. After that, the place loses its allure and they look for somewhere else to live and explore. They leave right when most newcomers are finding their feet and getting settled.

Brief honeymoon

As for me, when I moved to Oregon, I had a brief honeymoon period. We were in rental accommodations for the first six months, and with no remodeling to do and little to unpack (most of our belongings were in storage), I had more free time to explore Portland. I began to experience the wonderful, eclectic things my city had to offer, like its markets, art, music scene, and cuisine. However, when the gorgeous summer months turned to the rainy, cold days of fall, the honeymoon ended. I became ill with chronic pain and had little energy to continue exploring the area or making friends. Then there was loneliness, coupled with the sense of loss and being lost that I described in the opening of this book.

Welcoming Ways

There are numerous ways we can feel less lost and transition from the unfamiliar to the familiar. I call this bridge building. Just as it can help to say farewell to our previous home, it can also be beneficial to say hello to the new one. In the same way that goodbye rituals announce that we're leaving, welcome traditions tell neighbors, and ourselves, that we're here now. They mark a fresh beginning. As Reverend Tinney said in his 2008 sermon on transitions, "These old rites of passage created clear points of separation between the past and the future . . . and provided a point of re-entry and a new beginning."

Have a housewarming

In western countries, the tradition of housewarming provides such a point of re-entry. Some say that the term "housewarming" may have originated from the act of literally warming a house: new neighbors would bring gifts of firewood and build fires in the hearth for warmth.

These days, housewarming usually takes the form of a party. This could be an "open house" in which guests can arrive anytime during a fixed period. Each guest could be asked to bring a potluck dish to share. It doesn't have to be elaborate; even a casual invitation for coffee, dessert, drinks, or snacks would serve the same purpose. It's a great way to meet neighbors and others.

When my parents relocated us back to India, when I was eight, we had an amazing housewarming party. It was similar to a block party in the West, with a colorful canopy in the street. It's typically referred to as *griha pravesh*, which means "entering the new home." We gave our house a name and a priest blessed all who entered.

There are many such traditions worldwide—you don't have to follow these, but you could come up with your own. Whatever your beliefs, it's heartwarming to welcome yourself in some way.

A welcome from strangers

When we first relocated to America from England, we got a surprise welcome from strangers. We were at a restaurant at the time and our children were little: Nikita was an eighteen-month-old baby and Vinnie was nearly four years old. It took ages for our food to arrive and when it finally did, the kids were too tired to eat it. We had to ask to have it packed to go. But when I went to pay, I was amazed to discover that the family at the other table had already paid for it. They refused to take the money from me and said, "Welcome to America!" I think it was more a welcome to the hospitality of the Midwest. I couldn't believe it!

My husband was waiting outside in the car with the children. When I told him what happened, he questioned their motives. Coming from London where people are reserved toward strangers, we were not accustomed to this level of friendliness.

Put out a welcome mat

If no one welcomes you, don't let it bother you; you can greet yourself. Other than throwing a house party, you can welcome yourself by planting something in the yard or in some pots. It will greet you every time you see it. The Sharmas, our friends in Michigan who became our surrogate family, welcomed us with a gift card to a local garden center. I used it to buy hyacinth bulbs and other plants. Usually I don't grow anything in our garden (other than weeds!) because of our track record of not staying long enough to enjoy the fruits of my labors. In this case, though, I was able to. Growing plants—in a garden, on a balcony, or even in a pot inside—is like laying out a colorful, living welcome mat. It helps you put down roots and claim the property as yours. As dogs mark their territory, we can too.

Personalize the place

Personalizing a home from the moment you arrive is as important as depersonalizing it before leaving. Samantha Sharma, the friend who gave me the gift card for the garden center, also encouraged me to hang up pictures to make my place more homey. Just as we tone down unique décor and other personal touches before selling a home, we need to add our own mark again when we move into the next one. When my daughter was two, she did exactly that! Mischievously, she used red crayon to decorate the white walls of our rental property, marking her territory and creating a sense of home for herself. It's not as easy for us adults to do, especially people like me who've moved frequently and lack roots. However, I wish I'd done this sooner to my current house, because it feels like it still belongs to the previous owner. What makes it worse is that we keep on receiving her mail!

Know your neighbors

Neighbors have sometimes welcomed me with a gift or card that includes their contact information. A few neighbors have invited me over for coffee. Others have been very unfriendly or not acknowledged me at all, even when I was eight months pregnant! But I usually managed to develop a cordial relationship with even the coldest of them. In fact, after a while, they would become attached to my family and me and be sorry to see us leave! It goes to show that there's always hope if you encounter these kinds of people.

If neighbors haven't approached you, try not to take it personally: there's usually a reason for it, and they may be quite friendly when you get to know them. When I first arrived in Indiana, I didn't see the neighbors on either side for most of the summer. I was beginning to assume that I had lousy neighbors. As it turned out, one of them was away spending time with her mother, who was dying. The other was away helping with her family's business. They were both sincerely apologetic about not being available to welcome and assist me. Our friendship grew and one of them eventually became the best neighbor I've ever had.

I strongly recommend getting to know neighbors quickly. A neighbor can be a great go-to person. This is someone you can ask basic questions of such as where to buy certain items or when trash is collected, or can turn to for other forms of support (more about this in chapter 6).

Getting Involved Locally

Become a resident again

People who have the most successful transitions become involved with the local community as soon as possible. Attend local events, join your local library, listen to local radio, watch local TV channels, shop at your neighborhood stores, eat at neighborhood restaurants, and get to know your local area. All these things can help you feel like a resident again.

Once you've settled in, try not to forget how you felt in those early months, and treat other newcomers as you would've wanted to be treated. You can form a welcoming committee with other people who enjoy being hospitable at work, school, or in your neighborhood. Or you can simply welcome newcomers with a plate of cookies, a plant, or a card with your contact information inside.

Some residents are naturally more community-minded, like Katherine, who knew all the neighbors on her entire block. She once threw an ice cream social for her whole neighborhood! She likes to be invested in where she lives, and was once on her neighborhood board. But everything changed when she moved from her suburban community to urban, condo living in California. She says she had nothing she cared about or wanted to change anymore. It was all such a void. The next time Katherine moves, she intends to think more about the type of community she wants.

When Lisa, our frequent mover, relocated from England to America, she felt totally out of place. She didn't realize that going from a big city with a population of more than eight million to a city one-fifth that size would be such a drastic change. She says it would be hard enough to move to a smaller town in England, but to have the cultural differences on top of the size differences made the transition more difficult. What Lisa didn't realize at the time was that she was experiencing culture shock.

Understanding Culture Shock

The honeymoon phase is actually the first stage of culture shock, a term that Kalvero Oberg, a world-renowned anthropologist, first came up with to describe the changes experienced when we travel to or live in places very different from our own.

Once the excitement of the honeymoon period dies down and the dust settles, we sometimes enter the "crisis" stage of culture shock. What was once appealing can now cause distress, as the differences between the cultures become more obvious. This is also when the reality hits that we're here to stay. Then there is a sense of loss and disorientation. Soon after this, we can experience the "flight" stage of culture shock, when we might romanticize our previous home and hometown and want to run back to it.

My son Vinnie warns parents to look out for signs of this happening to their children at college. He says, "As a current college freshman, I can say that the transition is very interesting and powerful. Firstly, the 'honeymoon' idea that you've just arrived in utopia is very real, but doesn't last forever. Parents, even if your kid's first few weeks are going perfectly, keep checking in because the struggles will probably begin within the first month."

If you don't experience a honeymoon phase and your struggles start sooner, don't worry. You may have skipped straight to the crisis and flight stages of culture shock—what I call homesickness. If this is the case, know that what you're going through is normal. Any negative feelings should subside, and you'll eventually become less isolated and adjust to living in the new location. The following chapter about overcoming homesickness will show you how.

Home

The new green roof
Shiny windows
And hardwood floors
Are not home.
Home is the life lived
Within those walls
That you pack with you
In your heart
When you move
To another place.

Kiran Prasad

Chapter 4

Overcoming Homesickness

Home is not where you live, but where they understand you.
CHRISTIAN MORGENSTERN

I shadowed the move of Raj, a young British man, who relocated to Canada to marry his fiancée. Five weeks after moving, he had a strange experience. It happened when he was at work one day. It was a slow afternoon, and he started browsing British websites to catch up on news and sports. For a while, he completely forgot where he was; it wasn't until someone walked in and started speaking in a Canadian accent that it all came back to him.

He says it was like waking up from a dream or hearing about someone passing away. It overwhelmed him to the point that he couldn't hear what the person was saying. He'd never experienced anything like that before. Then it really hit home: he was here to stay. He says the feeling was surreal and hard to describe. It stayed with him for days. Then, during a Skype call to family that weekend, he found himself getting really emotional. Seeing them all together over there while he was here . . . the reality kicked in.

Denise, a homemaker, experienced something similar after she relocated across the country from Michigan to California. She described a moment that was particularly difficult for her. It was during a lunch break at work when she was talking to her sister on the phone. Her sister was losing her house, and Denise wanted to help. She offered to come over after work, then burst into tears because it hit her that she couldn't just "come over." She didn't live three miles away anymore—she lived three thousand miles away! Denise was crying not only because she couldn't go to her sister's house, but because, for a few seconds, she thought she was home.

We've just seen some examples of the crisis stage of culture shock: the initial excitement has worn off, and reality hits that you're here to stay. Feelings of grief such as sadness, anger, regret, confusion, or doubt can take over, and the difference between cultures becomes apparent.

Taking Flight

After feeling this way for a while, you might enter the flight stage of culture shock. I refer to the crisis and flight stages collectively as homesickness because it's the feeling that most overwhelms us at this time. It's okay to feel this way. It's natural to be homesick; you're not alone.

After relocating across the country to New York, Melanie, a cancer survivor, was pining for her previous place. In a Facebook post, she wrote that she was clicking her ruby slippers together like Dorothy from *The Wizard of Oz*, saying, "Oh, Toto, there's no place like home!"

Although it's tempting to return to the place we left behind, it's best to wait at least six months. Transition experts tell us that this is the minimum time it takes to overcome the effects of culture shock. The same can be said for family and friends visiting us. When they leave, we have to disconnect from them again, which can take us a step back in our transition. It's something you have to decide for yourself because each person's circumstances are unique. Seeing familiar faces might be just what you need.

Some colleges actually discourage freshmen from going home for Thanksgiving because it's too soon after moving in. This recommendation was given to us, and although I was desperate to see my children for the holidays, I knew it was better to let them settle in.

Clear symptoms of homesickness

In her book *Raising Global Nomads*, Robin Pascoe points out that at this stage in a move, "if running away is not an option, then hiding out can seem like the perfect solution." A bed can provide that refuge, as it did for me, and as I describe at the start of this book. Homesickness entails clear symptoms such as crying and aches and pains. It can come and go in waves, and, like a huge wave, it can knock us off our feet. Psychologist and homesickness expert Dr. Christopher Thurber defines it as "half anxiety, half depression," in Julie Bosman's 2007 *New York Times* article, "When There's No Place Like Home." He explains that while we can control the intensity of homesickness, we can't really prevent it.

Relocation depression

Psychologists tell us that homesickness can turn into "adjustment disorder," or situational depression, as it's commonly known. This is a short-term form of depression unlike clinical depression. It develops when we're finding it difficult to transition through a stressful situation, such as relocation. Once we've adjusted to the situation, these feelings should subside. If they don't, please seek professional help.

There's no shame in admitting we're having trouble adjusting. There's an epidemic of depression in Western society, yet too few people seek treatment because of the stigma attached to it. In America, the National Alliance on Mental Illness (NAMI) is working to fight the stigma and provides a reputable website and forums for information and support. There are also relocation depression forums online. It's important not to feel alone.

Searching for Home

No longer home

It's ironic—even though we're homesick for "our" home, it isn't ours anymore and it may not even exist in the way we remember it. Whenever a previous neighbor tells me about the alterations the new owners have made to my house, it's a rude awakening. It's painful to hear that the home we lovingly remodeled has been "gutted" and re-done. In Derrick Ho's 2010 CNN article, "Homesickness Isn't Really about 'Home,'" psychologist and professor Josh Klapow gets to the heart of homesickness. He says we're not literally missing our house; we're missing what's normal. He says homesickness stems from our "instinctive need for love, protection, and security—feelings and qualities usually associated with home."

What is home?

Buddhist master Thich Nhat Hanh, a world leader on mindfulness, believes that your true home is in the here and now. In my research about what home is, I discovered that most people say it's not a physical location but an emotional connection. Home is: where the heart is;

where your friends and family are; where you have un-conditional love; where you feel safe and secure; or where you can belong.

For many children, home is where their parents are. No matter where a parent or child moves to, parents are the safe harbor, or even the anchor, for their children. Reverend Kathleen admits that she didn't stop calling Iowa her home until her mother passed away. Home is where we have a sense of familiarity and where we've built memories.

Missing Friends, Family, Familiarity

After my brother relocated his family from England to Canada, he became aware of how the lack of friends, family, and familiarity can cause homesickness. He calls these the three F's of moving and jokes about how you'll want to use the "F" word when you're lacking these in your life! There's much that's unfamiliar, and we long for something familiar to connect with.

Make new memories

A sense of familiarity and connection comes when we have personal history or memories in a place, of precious times spent with family and friends in parts of our previous home and hometown—that's what made it special for us. This will happen again: give it time. Before we know it, we'll have fresh memories to fondly look back on. We just need to start making them.

My brother and his family did exactly that. Now, after years of living in Canada, he finally feels at home, that he belongs. One reason is because he's only recently become familiar with nearly every inch of his nearby surroundings. His family has taken each exit off the highway close to his children's school and explored it on foot, discovering walking trails.

Perhaps it's when we can go from being a tourist to a tour guide in our town that we are truly home. My brother now proudly tours his family and friends around the places he once found hard to connect with. He says he and his family are leaving behind a trail of footsteps and memories through which they are gradually falling in love with every part of their local area. This is heartwarming to hear, because he had such a difficult transition.

Grief Triggers

Our senses

Our strongest memories are evoked by our senses. After losing a loved one, any of the five senses can instantly beam us back to the life we left behind and trigger grief. A song or a word can do it; even a familiar scent. Every time I smell lilacs or hyacinths, I think of England, and the scents of lavender and lily of the valley remind me of my mom. Food evokes strong memories, too, since it can involve all five senses. Therefore, traditions involving food are painful for many of us.

Traditions

Traditions can be powerful triggers for grief, especially during major holidays, birthdays, and other important events shared with loved ones. For Melanie, a cancer survivor who moved from Detroit to New York City, the fond memory of celebrating Paczki Day threw her into a state of homesickness when that day of the year came around. In a Facebook post, she shared how no one she spoke to in New York that day had ever heard of eating a paczki for Fat Tuesday. I remember paczkis from when I lived in Michigan; they're Polish pastries similar to donuts. The traditional reason for making them was to use up lard, sugar, and other rich ingredients that are forbidden during Lent. They represent one last feast before the fasting season begins. Food memories are strong!

Like Melanie, certain traditions make me nostalgic. In England, Mother's Day is celebrated at a completely different time of the year than in America. I would always forget, and my family in England would have to remind me. Whenever British Mother's Day came around, no one in America was even aware of it, nor could I buy a card at that time. It always bothered me. This day has become more painful since my mother passed away.

Traditions and holiday celebrations are powerful grief triggers because it's tough to face the "firsts" of anything after a transition. It's natural to wish we could celebrate these occasions in the same way as before, with the same people. Instead, we have to accept that we can't and create new ones or fresh ways to celebrate them.

Most experts agree that it takes at least a year to adjust to a move. This makes sense because once we've been through a year's cycle of celebrations, it becomes easier to feel at home. Therefore, don't underestimate how long it takes to adjust or expect too much of yourself. Allow plenty of time to get grounded, and look at the progress you're making each week. We all grieve in our own way and own time, so don't compare your response to anyone else's. Be good to yourself and practice self-care when something triggers grief.

Things that might help

- Practice deep breathing techniques.

- Listen to relaxation music, meditate, or do guided visualization (where someone or a video or CD takes you step by step through how to bring your body to a relaxed state).

- Go for a walk or do something physical, like gardening.

- Find a creative outlet like music, art, cooking, dance, or writing.

- Write letters that you won't send, or keep a journal about how you're feeling. Give a name to those feelings and express them. Write as if you're talking to a friend.

- If you're angry and resentful about the move, express those feelings in a healthy way. Then try to forgive the person or circumstances that caused you to relocate.

- Be around caring people who know how you feel. Talk to a grief counselor or life coach, or join a grief support group. Find a healthy outlet for these emotions.

Attachment and Impermanence

Although the suggestions listed above might help soothe our suffering, it's also important to understand how suffering comes about and how changing our perspective can lessen it. Buddhist philosophy teaches us how we cause our own suffering by becoming attached to impermanent things. Although we know nothing lasts forever, we still cling to people, objects, and even our health and youth. In his book *The Ultimate Happiness Prescription*, spiritual guru Deepak Chopra tells us that our tendency to rely on external things such as friends, family, and familiar places can cause suffering when they're taken away.

Timber Hawkeye, a modern monk and author of *Buddhist Boot Camp*, shares this in his chapter on permanence: "In my twenties I got a tattoo at the end of each one of my relationships. I think it's because I was disappointed and looking for something permanent when everything else felt uncertain." He goes on to write, "Are we all looking for something permanent in an impermanent world? The moment we accept, not fear, that everything is temporary, we can appreciate each breath as a gift. Whether it's the love of a friend, our family, youth, or life itself, let's celebrate and enjoy that we have it here today."

Letting Go

The idea of letting go is fundamental to Buddhism; to live each moment without getting attached to it. It helps us accept that if our loved ones or something we love were to disappear tomorrow, our world wouldn't collapse. Most recently, my greatest loss has been the loss of my mother and her unconditional love. I feel nothing can replace it. I yearn for her loving touch, voice, and physical presence. It's not easy, but I have to let go of the way things were and accept that life will never be the same again.

Resist the allure of the past

Long after we've physically moved away, we can find ourselves clinging to people and organizations that were once a part of our life. We want to believe we're indispensable to them. My neighbor Leslie said that after she arrived in Portland, she continued to receive emails from her children's previous school and her book club. She wanted to think that their lives couldn't go on without her, or at least that they couldn't be having as much fun without her. My brother said the same about the friends he left behind in England. It was difficult for him to hear that they were continuing their social gatherings without him. Realizing we can be easily replaced is a bitter pill to swallow.

Sarah from Oregon stayed connected to previous friends virtually, through Facebook and email. She says that in some ways it actually didn't help at all. Another person, known as "Sam I Am" on a citydata.com forum, explains why the allure of the past is very strong. He tells us, "I've found that places we left and people who are gone reach a certain level of sainthood in our minds once we are separated from them, which isn't necessarily reality either. Be aware of what you might have built up in your mind as utopia with perfect Stepford people. Most likely it wasn't that way at all." He goes on to encourage us to try to remember why we left, because it's "easy to glaze over the less than perfect aspects and only remember the good. Utopian memories not based in reality can interfere with our growth in new relationships."

Changing Your Attitude

Avoid negative assumptions

While we rose-tint the past, we do the opposite to our present situation. The qualities we found endearing in people and things during the honeymoon period can become less endearing after living there for a while.

At this stage, we also find ourselves making assumptions based on single encounters or experiences. If we meet one unhelpful person, we stereotype everyone as the same. I did this when we first moved to Portland and my son's car broke down outside a house a few blocks away. A couple of ladies were chatting outside their homes and didn't bother asking if he needed help. I thought, *They are so unhelpful. Our new neighborhood is hostile.* Then I started comparing it to my previous town, which seemed perfect in comparison. A few years later, we thought differently when my husband's car got stuck in the snow as he was leaving for the airport. We were amazed at how many neighbors showed up to help push it. I've since learned that it's unfair to judge a place based on our initial impressions of a few people, or compare it to where we used to live. What we condemned about a culture because it was foreign, we can later come to accept.

Highlight the positives

When we only remember the good things about our former place and focus on the bad things about the new, it keeps us stuck in the past. What if we could do the opposite? By highlighting the positives about our current location, we can shift our perspective to a present-oriented one. My daughter is naturally good at looking at the bright side of things. She says, "I've told myself throughout moves, *You're not 'losing' old friends. In fact, you aren't really losing anything.* I look at it like I'm simply expanding my memories, experiences, and friends. It may be a tough mindset to get into at first, but it's never failed in keeping me positive and happy in my previous moves."

Be grateful

We can be positive by taking stock of all that's wonderful about our present situation, or by appreciating what we've gained or still have. Do it right now. Make a list of everything that's right about your new home, city, and community, as though you were a realtor about to sell it to others. What would you say if you had no comparison? I did that with my current home (which I've struggled to connect with). It made me aware of many things I'd overlooked or taken for granted. I found it made me more grateful for what I have. The loss felt from one life can be filled with fresh things if we open ourselves to it. English poet William Cowper says it well: "Oh, my friend, it's not what they take away from you that counts. It's what you do with what you have left." It's not easy, although it's certainly possible to take on this perspective, even in the direst of circumstances.

I was at a Haitian benefit dinner one evening and got talking to a wonderful woman named Judith Gelin, of Portland's Society of Haitian Arts and Culture. She'd just returned from helping with the Haiti earthquake relief efforts, and she told me about the experiences of the female refugees. Many of these women had lost their husbands or children, as well as their homes. Yet they stood under cover of a temporary shelter and said they were happy, and beamed beautiful smiles. They explained to her how it's the Haitian way to be grateful for what you have left. I can't imagine how it must feel to go through such extreme loss and displacement. However, these women found a way to cope. We can learn from the Haitian mindset that it's possible to maintain hope in almost any situation.

Maintain hope

Hope is an essential element in the moving process, and in life. If you lose hope, you lose your will to carry on because you can't put a positive spin on the situation. You can't see a light at the end of the tunnel. A few times when I went through dark times, I lost hope. It devastated me, affecting my health and my family. As much as I tried, I couldn't see how I'd ever feel positive about where I'd relocated to or replace what I'd lost. Without a job, friendship, support, a house I loved, a sense of belonging, and my health, I was truly lost.

Some people turn to religion or spirituality for relief when things become bleak, but at the time, I had no church or spiritual center to attend. There was also little support material out there. Other than the books by Robin Pascoe, one book I found really comforting was Susan Miller's *After the Boxes are Unpacked*. She shows many ways to maintain hope during a difficult relocation. She does this through a belief in God and the Bible. Even though I don't share the same religious beliefs as Susan, her words gave me comfort because she truly understands how it feels to go through this.

The Neutral Time

Why is this part of a move so challenging? In an article called "The Important Difference between Change and Transition," organizational change consultant Jeff Bracken writes that "metaphorically, this is that in-between stage when you have let go of one trapeze, and you have not yet grasped the other trapeze that you hope is coming your way!"

You might notice that your previous friends contact you less or not at all. Their lives go on without you and they expect yours to do the same. If you don't yet have friends or somewhere to belong, you can be left drifting and lonely in this neutral time. In *Transitions: Making Sense of Life's Changes*, William Bridges describes this feeling as "floating free in a kind of limbo between two worlds," or being suspended in time between the old life and new life as a "rudderless boat."

To me, it feels like being stuck in the middle of a bridge, unable to cross to either side. It reminds me of a family trip to Niagara Falls: if you stand in the middle of the bridge above the falls, you can have one foot in Canada and the other in America. We thought it was amusing to stand in the middle, with both feet together in no man's land. It's not as amusing when you're experiencing this on an emotional level! When you have one foot in each community, you can remain stuck in the middle of the bridge, neither here nor there.

Stepping Forward

Invest emotionally

To cross the bridge to the other side, you have to take steps in the right direction. This requires a lot of emotional energy, and it can leave you drained. Among other things, you have to become established again in a school, workplace, or neighborhood. It takes time to do that and we can become frustrated until we do.

After our move to Indiana, my son, a teenager at the time, wished there was a way to speed up the process. He didn't like feeling unsettled. At first, he refused to emotionally invest in his environment, saying this was only his temporary home until he moved to college. For the first year, he avoided getting close to anyone and wouldn't invite acquaintances over to know them better. He was still angry about having to leave friends behind in Michigan—ones he'd known since kindergarten. By the time he eventually invested in these relationships, it was time for us to leave again!

It's best not to let a time frame dictate getting to know people. Even short-term relationships can lead to long-term ones and give us much-needed support.

Facing Uncertainty

Accept the now

In times of uncertainty, we're tempted to look back at the past, where we felt more secure, and want it back. Drifting in a sea of the unknown with nothing to anchor us can make us feel disoriented, powerless, fearful, or even angry. While we can't control the people and events around us, it's empowering to know that we can control how we respond to those events. I love the serenity prayer that says, "God, grant me the serenity to accept the things I cannot change, the courage to change the things I can, and the wisdom to know the difference."

Deepak Chopra also talks about acceptance in his book *Ageless Body, Timeless Mind.* He has a whole chapter devoted to the wisdom of uncertainty. In it, he tells us that there are two ways to cope with uncertainty: acceptance or resistance. He says it's unhealthy to resist. Carl Jung, the founder of analytical psychology, would agree—one of his famous quotes is, "What you resist persists."

Mindfulness meditation can help us come to a healthy acceptance of uncertainty. I practice it myself and find it to be successful. I use the affirmation "I am here now" and repeat it silently in my head when my thoughts divert to certainties of the past or uncertainties of the future. In *Stillness Speaks*, Eckhart Tolle explains how "this one moment—Now—is the only thing you can never escape from, the one constant factor in your life. No matter what happens, no matter how much your life changes, one thing is certain: it's always Now. Since there is no escape from the Now, why not welcome it, become friendly with it?" He adds, "When you make friends with the present moment, you feel at home no matter where you are. When you don't feel at home in the Now, no matter where you go, you will carry unease with you."

Give it time

I believe that one of the reasons we feel happy at the start of the honeymoon phase is because we're fully in the present moment. If we continue to do things mindfully, we're better able to maintain that feeling or re-create it at any time. Whatever our initial response to somewhere, it helps if we stay present and accept it for what it is. Give the place at least six months—longer if you can. Postpone any major decisions during this time because people tend to have difficulty thinking clearly then. Who knows? It might grow on you. Anywhere can become home if you want it to.

When my son was a student, he had this encouraging message to share about his transition to college: "The feeling that college life is alien does go away eventually.

As a second-semester freshman, I can safely say that the university I attend is a true home."

Carrying Our Home

A few months ago, I was sitting in the middle of Union Square in San Francisco. I was basking in the warm sunshine when out of the blue, I got thinking about how lucky a turtle is to be able to carry its home with it everywhere, in the form of its shell. What if we could do that too? I believe we can, only our real home is *within* us. We just have to become aware of it and connect with it to find true joy. Internally, a feeling of home is when we can feel at home with ourselves. It's when we're centered and in balance and our emotional needs are being met. In part two, I'll show you how we can do this. Chapters 5 to 9 collectively represent the connection phase and what we have to do to feel at home again.

Part Two

Feel at Home Again:

Connection Phase

Searching

I sit searching...searching....
On my laptop
For something to complete me.
Maybe a job, a course....
What is it I'm after?
I wish I knew
So that I could find it.
Something I must do
Something I must contribute
Before I leave.
And each new year mocks me
That I'm still not there.

Kiran Prasad

Chapter 5

Neediness

*You will be your best self when you take time to understand what
you really need, feel, and want.*

DEBORAH DAY

I've often wondered why we become so needy after relocating. We have a heightened need to make friends, be loved, feel safe, belong, be acknowledged . . . the list goes on and on. Then I discovered something that might offer an explanation: the "hierarchy of needs," a theory of human behavior and motivation by psychologist Abraham Maslow.

Happiness and Motivation

Surprisingly, Maslow's work on happiness and motivation stemmed from a sad, frustrated life. In an online biography written for Muskingum University, Michelle Emrich tells us that Maslow's mother was unloving and insensitive and his father was physically and emotionally unavailable. In fact, his father hated him and degraded him in public. He pushed Maslow to excel in things he wasn't interested in.

This might partly explain why Maslow didn't do well in school, even dropping out at one point, although he was highly gifted. He felt socially isolated as a Jewish boy in a non-Jewish community, and he grew up unhappy and without friends. Fortunately, Maslow's life improved in later years. He went on to develop a sense of purpose and optimism that would inspire him to study motivation and happiness in others. It finally led to the theories he's known for today.

Hierarchy of Needs

Maslow is best known for his hierarchy of needs theory, which basically says that we have needs that can be ranked. It's sad and not surprising that the hierarchy includes things that Maslow was missing in his own life. He explains the theory in his book *Motivation and Personality*, portraying the needs as layers that form a pyramid. However, for my purposes, I'm depicting this pyramid as the roof of a house to show how these needs relate to feeling at home again.

Applying Maslow to Moving

The bottom of the roof represents our most basic *physiological* needs, followed by our needs for *safety, love and/or belonging, esteem,* and *self-actualization*. Later, Maslow added three more needs to the hierarchy: between esteem and self-actualization, he put *cognitive* needs and *aesthetic* needs. He split self-actualization into two parts, adding *self-transcendence* to the top of the pyramid. He then grouped them into deficiency and growth needs.

Deficiency needs

- **Physiological** needs for things that are crucial to survival, such as air, food, and water.
- **Safety** needs, including those for shelter, security, and order.
- **Love/Belonging** needs for friendship, intimacy, and connection.
- **Esteem** needs to achieve and gain approval.

Growth needs

- **Cognitive** needs, or the desire to know and understand.
- **Aesthetic** needs for form, beauty, and balance in our surroundings.
- **Self-actualization** needs to realize our true potential and find self-fulfillment.
- **Self-transcendence** needs to help others realize their potential.

When we relocate, we spend more time trying to satisfy deficiency needs. And indeed, Maslow's theory is that if basic needs aren't met first, we won't be interested in growth needs like self-actualization.

Although psychologists today debate about whether or not these needs are in fact strictly hierarchical, this theory has helped me understand why certain things were important to me at particular stages of my many relocations. It made me realize why I always feel like I'm back at square one each time I move—it's because it takes a lot of energy and stamina to start this process all over again.

During my move to Oregon, I became very aware of these needs and made notes about them. Fortunately, my physiological needs were never in danger of going unfulfilled. Shelter was the priority, and I became quite anxious when, three days before we had to leave Indiana, we still hadn't found a short-term rental property that would allow a dog. Surprising in a dog-friendly state like Oregon!

Once we found accommodation, I became preoccupied with stocking the refrigerator and pantry with basic necessities such as bread and milk. I got referrals from the neighbors for the best grocery stores. Then my need for order took over as I tried to arrange and rearrange things. After that, I wanted to find a gym and medical services for my family so we could stay healthy and fit.

Once all those were fulfilled, it was important to belong. I became concerned about whether my children were fitting in at school and how I was fitting into my neighborhood and community. A little after that, self-esteem took the forefront and I started job-hunting. Eventually, when we were more settled, self-actualization became important. I wanted to be valued for my contribution to something—I wanted to make a difference in the world. I thought about doing various things, but what I most desired was to complete this book, get it published, and help people struggling with a difficult move. I was one needy person! Add to that the fact that my family members all had their own needs and it's no wonder that transitioning to a new life is exhausting.

Our desires often change dramatically after we relocate. This can have an impact on relationships, especially if our needs conflict with those of our loved ones. For example, having given up jobs a number of times, I was reluctant to become a homemaker again when we relocated to Portland. Unfortunately, I had little choice because the economy had slumped and school districts were cutting back on teachers, especially reading specialists like me. Then, when I became chronically ill, I had no option at all. Everyone else in the family was busy with school or work demands, which meant I got little help from them. This left me resentful about being put in the position of homemaker again. I didn't have much of their company, either. Therefore, I needed friends and somewhere to belong more than ever before. It's important to take stock of your needs and take positive steps to fulfill them.

Children's Needs

Michael Thompson, Catherine O'Neill-Grace, and Lawrence Cohen write in *Best Friends, Worst Enemies: Understanding the Social Lives of Children* that the most important needs for children are connection, recognition, and power. This goes along with what I believe: that at each step of a move, children should be allowed to have some say. How much power they're given depends on their age and maturity, but they can be included in choosing a house and school, deciding what to give away, how to decorate their room, which extracurricular activities to take up, and (within reason) who they choose as friends.

The Needs of Accompanying Partners

Relocation coach Maripat Abbott uses Maslow's hierarchy and a five-step process to support executives and their spouses as they prepare for and go through a move. In a 2014 article on her blog titled "Maslow's Hierarchy of Relocation," she explains that just because the closing papers are signed on a house, it doesn't mean that the first level of the pyramid is satisfied. Sure, there's a real home to move to and food, water, and warmth, but "there is an irrational fear of feeling like nowhere is home, of feeling displaced. If not addressed, this fear can impact [ou]r ability to move forward and ever feel at home and safe in the new location."

Abbott stresses the importance of checking in with the accompanying spouse about their feelings, because the spouse might not even be aware that these needs are being threatened. After the basic needs are met, the accompanying spouse and family can comfortably begin to transition forward and assimilate into a neighborhood. Abbott explains, "Ultimately, the goal is to be in the new zip code and begin to experience true fulfillment, the pinnacle of Maslow's model."

In the following chapters we will be looking in more depth at these needs: how to connect to a new neighborhood and home, and how to eventually find true fulfillment.

The Driver's Seat

I was lost in my life
Going from day to day
Without a destination
So I looked back
At where I had come from
And mapped out
Where I wanted to go.
It gave my life direction
And put me back in
The driver's seat.

Kiran Prasad

Chapter 6

Safety

The ache for home lives in all of us. The safe place where we can go as we are and not be questioned.

MAYA ANGELOU

After we have a roof over our heads and have satisfied our most critical needs, safety becomes a priority. This includes security, order, law, limits, stability, and protection from the elements. I include health here as well. Fulfilling our safety needs is, as Maslow explains in *Motivation and Personality*, "providing a bumper or airbags on a car; while you don't always need them, having them gives you some confidence that you can face minor bumps and bruises along the road of life."

Protecting Yourself from the Elements

Be prepared

Being prepared for the climate you're moving to is crucial—I can't tell you how many people, including myself, have been surprised by the new climate they faced. Vinod, a young man who recently moved from California to Oregon, admits that although he knew it was green in Oregon, he didn't know how much it rained. He didn't ask anyone about the climate before he got there, and when he arrived in Portland for a job interview, the weather was great and everything looked lush, unlike dry San Diego where he lived. He says he'd never owned a rain jacket in his life; he'd never even considered it. Vinod is originally from India and says that when it rains there, no one goes out. He hadn't driven in rain or snow before, and found it quite challenging. His manager had to help him by teaching him things like how to put snow chains on his tires. Vinod never thought the weather could affect his life so much.

It was the same for me. When I first moved to America, it was January and snowing heavily in Michigan. We were living in an extended stay hotel near a busy intersection. I was already worried about having to drive on the "wrong" side of the road; the snow only made it worse. I'd never driven in these conditions and wasn't used to driving a huge minivan, either—I'd always had tiny cars in England. Nor had I passed the U.S. driving test or even looked at the manual yet. Add to that the fact that I had a baby and an active toddler with me, and it's no surprise that I was anxious about driving!

Consequently, for those first couple of months of winter, I didn't drive at all. This meant I was confined to our small space with two kids all day. It drove me crazy because they weren't in school and our shipment of their toys and things hadn't arrived yet. My husband would come home and say, "Why didn't you go out with the kids? Why aren't you driving? I got you a car." I felt like throttling him! He just didn't understand; he's comfortable driving anywhere in the world. I was very dependent on him for those few months.

Seek medical advice

The weather can affect us emotionally, too. Vinod says he couldn't understand why he felt so tired and down after relocating to Oregon. Then he realized that the lack of sun, especially compared to the other places he'd lived, was really affecting him. Seasonal affective disorder (SAD) is common in this part of the world— it's a type of depression that occurs with seasonal changes in light. One of the treatments for it is light therapy, using a special lamp. I'll tell you more about this later in the chapter, but please seek medical advice if you think you've developed SAD or if the climate is affecting you adversely.

Help pets face the climate

Pets face their own challenges with the changes in weather. Some start shedding more, which is what happened to our dog. In fact, I was shedding along with him! The stress of relocating was making my hair fall out. (Luckily, I have plenty of it.)

Jill, a friend of ours from Indiana, shared her experience of transporting pets across the country and how they coped with the weather. She described how they had to take their pets in separate vehicles: cats in one, dog in the other. She said they recently had snow for the first time since they moved. The dog they brought over from Indiana loved it, while the dog they acquired while in North Carolina was less than thrilled.

Feeling Secure

Keep familiar items close

It helps if children as well as pets can travel to the destination with their favorite bedding, dishes, and something for recreation. That way, when they arrive they'll already feel comfortable. Just as a puppy feels happier if sent to a foreign place wrapped in a familiar blanket and scent, adults might too.

Allie from Atlanta tells me that she unpacks the most familiar items first, like curtains and bedspreads. She lays those out quickly. Since most things get shuffled around in boxes and she's often too tired to figure things out on arrival, she packs things very carefully. She puts the last items used at the top for easy access at the other end of the move—that way, she can put them out first. This helps her feel like everything's familiar in the bedroom, kitchen, etc. It helps her feel secure.

Psychologists Marcia Hausman and James Reed explain in their 1991 article, "Psychological Issues in Relocation: Response to Change" that "those who find ways to establish security and meaning in their new situation within a reasonable time (two to six months) will suffer less turmoil." One way I establish security and meaning is to quickly set up ways to communicate.

Set up modes of communication

It's amazing these days how lost and insecure we feel, especially teenagers, without a cell phone and the Internet. Therefore, I make it a priority to get lines of communication reestablished. It's reassuring to children to connect with old friends when they don't have new ones yet. Phone information is also required for school and work forms.

In the days before FaceTime, Skype, and WhatsApp, I would sign up for an international calling plan through my home phone as well. With most of my family still in England, I made full use of that plan, speaking for hours when I missed them. I tried not to depend too heavily on the company of those far away, and I connected locally too.

It helped me feel safer by having the ability to block unwanted calls, I did this through my phone company. Then I added my cell and home phone numbers to the U.S. government's Do Not Call Registry for discouraging telemarketers. All of this will vary depending on where you live and who your phone provider is.

Connecting your TV is important too, so you can tune into the local news and become acclimated to your surroundings. When we first moved to America, we thought we'd only be here for a short work assignment. At first, we didn't bother buying major appliances like a TV. While it was great to take a break from TV and do better things with our time, we all missed out in some way. It meant we were less able to understand American references and popular culture, which further isolated us as foreigners.

Secure your finances

As foreigners in a new place, our finances can also be a source of stress. Whether our financial situation has worsened or improved, we need to update paperwork, including life, property, and car insurance, as well as banking information. If we have a will, that might need updating too.

Shortly after our arrival in America, I insisted that we set up a will and include information about who would have custody of our children and be the executor of our estate if something happened to us. When we're newcomers and have no real support system, we worry about many things.

Secure yourself medically

If you have children or pets, stock up on emergency medical items. It's important to ensure that your medical insurance is set up as well. Read the insurance plan, understand how it works, and know whether you have to stay within your plan's network of health providers. Also, get referrals for doctors, vets, and other medical services. Knowing the location of the closest hospital with an ER is critical.

Gather this information well before you need it: Moving seems to take its toll on a person's health, and you really don't want to be hunting for medical supplies and services when you or a loved one is ill. Do the same with security in general; equip yourself with safety information before you need it.

Feel secure in general

When Vinod lived in Texas, he didn't feel safe walking alone at night in downtown Dallas. He says he felt uncomfortable after 10P.M. and worried about being mugged. When going downtown in the evening, he felt more comfortable being with others.

It's understandable to feel this way when you're unfamiliar with a territory. You don't yet know which parts of your town are safe, so everywhere can feel unsafe. You might even feel unsafe in your own house for a while—the unfamiliar sounds of a home at night can be unnerving at first.

There are numerous things you can do to feel secure at home, starting with some simple emergency-preparedness measures:

- Find phone numbers for the local police, fire department, utility companies, and other emergency services and put the list on the refrigerator for easy access.
- Make a note of the closest urgent care centers and hospitals, for both pets and humans.
- Know where all the shutoff valves are for your home's utilities, especially gas and water.
- Know neighbors' phone numbers and put up a list of emergency people that you or your children could contact, including school numbers. Make sure everyone in the family knows where the list is located and that your kids know their home phone number and address.
- Get spare house keys made, with one spare hidden outside or in the garage if you have no one to entrust it to.
- Buy fire extinguishers as soon as possible (moving companies don't normally allow you to transport those).
- Make sure you have smoke detectors and carbon monoxide detectors installed immediately. They are vital, as we discovered.

How we nearly died!

Carbon monoxide detectors (and my great sense of smell!) saved my family's life in our first week in a rental house. I thought I could smell gas one night, so we slept with all the windows open. Although carbon monoxide is odorless, fortunately for us it was mixed with other gases. To see if we had a leak, we bought a couple of carbon monoxide detectors. Sure enough, the detectors warned us that we did. It was a frightening experience, with the alarms going off in the middle of the night. They were flashing red, confirming high levels of the gas that can kill you in your sleep. My landlady later sent a service person out to confirm this. We were lucky we detected it in time!

Getting Your Bearings

Outside the security of our home, we can get lost and off-course. Therefore, it's important to become familiar with our surroundings as soon as possible. We can do this in various ways: learning about the culture, getting to know the community, and finding our way around the neighborhood. If we went on a pre-visit to look at schools and houses, we might have a general idea of where everything is. Now we'll need to navigate more specifically.

Use a navigation device

When I moved to Portland, I experienced what inevitably comes with being in a new city: getting lost. To make matters worse, I have a terrible sense of direction—it often keeps me from venturing far. Before getting here, a couple of friends suggested I buy a navigation device. My husband had suggested this a number of times too, yet I was reluctant to put much faith in a machine.

Thank goodness I did. As a newcomer in town, it was a lifesaver! I used it for house hunting, finding local shops, getting to social events, and exploring the area. Technology has come far since then. These days, I use a navigation app on my iPhone.

Have a go-to person

Just like we need a map or navigation device for the new territory, we also need a "go-to" person (a neighbor or colleague at work, for example) to help us navigate through life. It's natural to feel lost and off-course in both our physical environment and our emotional state after a relocation. There's a lot that's foreign and out of our control. When I interviewed people for my book, I found that the most successful movers had great support systems.

Neighbors as go-to people

Some of the best go-to people can be your neighbors. I can't stress enough how important it is to introduce yourself to them early; you never know when you'll need their support. You can list them as an emergency contact for your family and your children's school, get referrals from them for medical services, and ask them for advice on where to buy things. It always gave me peace of mind to know I had somebody dependable close by, especially since my husband was sometimes out of town right after we relocated!

In the first week of moving to Indiana, we got into a difficult situation and had to turn to a neighbor for help. We'd been busy unpacking, and I decided that we should take a break. We stepped outside on the deck without our shoes on. As I closed the patio door, I discovered that we had locked ourselves out! (The door had a built-in automatic lock.)

I had to walk barefoot to a neighbor's house for help. Although the Yagers had only met me once, they invited me inside to call a locksmith. They even offered to let me wait in their home while they went out to run an errand!

(I felt too uncomfortable to take them up on that.) Luckily, it was a warm summer day and we were soon back inside our home. We laughed about the incident later.

Help your pets acclimate

If you're moving to a completely different type of environment, such as from the suburbs to the city, or from a quiet neighborhood to a noisy one, your pet might be affected by it.

Our dog, Jasper, had never been a barker, but in our Oregon rental house he started to bark every night at something outside. Our neighbor said it could be coyotes or rats lurking there. We were only used to squirrels and rabbits in our previous yard, so this was disconcerting. Jasper, our overly friendly dog, became more and more territorial and suspicious; he would bark crazily at everyone. Then my landlady informed me of the public path that ran along the side of our garden. One day, I saw a lady walking her dog along it and her dog defecated on our grass! Jasper was going out of his mind, as was I. No wonder he was behaving territorially.

Pet routines

Try to keep pets' routines, such as walks and playtime, consistent. It makes them feel secure. Just as you would with children, avoid making too many changes to their food, toys, or bedding, at least for the first months. They've already faced lots of upheaval during relocation—when we moved from Indiana to Oregon, our dog had to endure a seven-day road trip and be boarded at both ends of the move.

Recognize separation anxiety

Watch for signs of stress in your pets or trouble adjusting. Stress can sometimes cause the pet to display something called "separation anxiety" when left alone. The American Society for the Prevention of Cruelty to Animals (ASPCA), states on their website that the symptoms of separation anxiety in dogs can include: urination or defecation indoors; barking; howling; chewing, digging, and destruction; pacing; or trying to escape.

In my dog's case, he showed his distress by over-grooming and over-marking his territory. Jasper would go for walks and urinate every few yards; he would even lift up his leg when there was nothing left to mark his territory with!

Bringing Back Order

Anchors have been weighed, and it can feel like you're drifting out to sea without a rudder or a life raft. Moving involves a lot of chaos and disequilibrium—life gets thrown completely out of balance. It's tough enough for the most organized among us, but if you're disorganized, it's an even greater challenge. It depends on what type of person you are. Do you prefer order, routines, and structure? Or are you more spontaneous? Either way, no one likes to live in complete chaos. Here are some ways to regain order.

Anchoring rituals

Have routines

It's not until you get into normal day-to-day routines that you'll experience what a place is actually like, especially if you're not working outside of the home. Routine brings normality and order to chaos. In her book *Will this Place Ever Feel Like Home?*, Leslie Levine explains that routine "tells us where we're going" and "offers us security, [and] moving interrupts those routines."

While old routines can help at first by acting as a bit of a crutch, later they might be replaced with new ones. Young children in particular need the comfort of routine and familiarity. Toddlers can get upset and feel lost when they're bombarded with too much change. They may express their agitation through regressive behaviors such as thumb-sucking; needing a pacifier, bottle, or "blankie" again; bed-wetting; or nightmares. Children of all ages can show their distress through behaviors such as clowning around, being aggressive or irritable, crying, having changes in appetite or sleep patterns, or displaying mood swings.

When we moved to a rental house in Michigan, my daughter, a preschooler at the time, was missing our previous house and kept drawing pictures of it. She also expressed concerns that she wouldn't be able to find her way around our new home. Both my children would show their agitation by getting into fights with each other or taking it out on me by not cooperating. It drove me mad!

To help children adjust quickly, keep to their routines: familiar foods and TV shows, reading to them before bed, and a set bedtime. Older kids can feel more secure by continuing the routine of playing organized sports or other extracurricular activities.

Anchoring rituals benefit adults, too. Since I wasn't always working outside the home, I spent afternoons at the library writing this book and maintained our routine of eating dinner together as a family at a set time.

Once the children's schedules became busier in high school, it was impossible for us to eat together regularly. Many of my son's soccer games were too early for my husband to attend with me, so I attended alone while my daughter stayed home to do homework. Another routine that changed was when my children learned to drive and didn't need me to shuttle them to school anymore. I lost even that structure to my day. At that point we all had new routines that we had to get used to, although even those could change from week to week. The meltdown in the shower that I described at the start of the book was partly brought on by my loss of routine and structure.

Get organized

It's a mammoth task to create order out of the chaos once the boxes are unpacked. Relocation coach Maripat Abbot says she hires people like professional organizers to do the jobs she feels are her weakness. If, like me, you prefer to organize things yourself, Julie Morgenstern's book, *Organizing from the Inside Out*, has wonderful tips for organizing your home. Here are two tips of my own:

- Unpack room by room or by category. We tend to unpack our bed and bedding first, followed by all the kitchen items.
- Prioritize and achieve one goal a day if more than that is too overwhelming. Make sure the goal or expectation is realistic.

Tools for organizing

How you organize your home will depend on your needs and priorities. For me, helping our children stay organized and taking control of our paperwork were the top priorities. Therefore, I bought a lot of organizing tools for those tasks. I set up a home office with paperwork organized into files, and I also prepared a study area for my kids, which had easy access to all their school supplies. Here are some of the tools I used:

- A portable accordion file. This is very handy for keeping important papers easily accessible at the start and end of a move. You can have sections like *house, job, school, classes,* and *clubs/organizations.*
- A daily to-do list or notebook. Split it into *to do, to buy,* and *to call.* Check off what you've achieved each day.
- Hanging files and folders.
- Address mailing labels.
- An address book or planner to note down contact information and referrals. Another option is to use a business card organizer or index-card box for referrals. (A smartphone or other device can store all this information electronically.)

Make new purchases gradually

I try not to rush into making too many new purchases at first. For one thing, until you've fully unpacked, it's difficult to know what you need. You might already have it in one of your boxes! I recommend purchasing things gradually—especially large items like furniture and appliances. Personally, I feel overwhelmed if I have to get used to operating many unfamiliar appliances at once. I don't enjoy plodding through those user manuals either. It's overwhelming, all the new things a person has to get used to at once.

Become familiar with new laws

Being organized includes becoming familiar with the laws most likely to affect you in a new country or state. When I first moved to America, I had a scary brush with the law. We were on a long road trip with my husband's family, who'd come to visit from England. We were going from Washington to New York in a large motor home, which I drove through the night while everyone slept.

As I was coming up to a major tunnel on the freeway, I saw signs warning about propane not being allowed through the tunnel. I ignored these warnings because I didn't think it concerned me. As I approached the entrance to the tunnel, a policeman signaled me to pull over. I'd never been stopped by a U.S. police officer before. It was unnerving, especially since he was armed with a gun! He got me to roll down my window and asked if I was carrying propane. I said no. Just then, my husband sleepily replied, "Yes we are."

I was used to calling propane "gas." The officer looked at me suspiciously, then took my license back to his vehicle. After a while, he returned and said he was letting me go with a warning. What a relief! After that, I reread my driver's manual thoroughly.

In America, laws vary by state. Therefore, every time we moved to another state, I had to relearn the "rules." For example, in Oregon it's illegal to pump your own gas at the gas station. I couldn't believe it at first; I thought a customer who informed me of it was joking! I had to get used to other laws as well, like those concerning employment, housing, pets, and children. There were whole new systems for doing things. It's worth doing some research before your move, since not knowing much about the legal system can cause anxiety.

Staying Healthy

Anxiety is only one of the health issues that affects people during relocation. Some people I interviewed also experienced migraines, mood changes, fatigue, and muscle pain brought on by tension. For me, the stress of my move to Oregon led to fibromyalgia, a chronic pain and fatigue syndrome. I went from being a fit person who worked out at the gym six days a week to someone who could barely walk and was in too much pain to even sit. My life as I knew it was over. Fortunately, I was able to improve my condition significantly by altering my diet and lifestyle. Now, I put my health first and encourage others to do the same.

Here are some successful strategies for taking good care of your health.

Get referrals and physicals

Get referrals for doctors, dentists, optometrists, and other specialists and schedule physicals or checkups upon arrival to make sure that all is okay with your health.

Check if you need supplements

Make sure you're stocked up with any nutritional supplements you might need, such as multivitamins or iron, because in times of stress they can be depleted. In climates where you get little sun, you might need to supplement with vitamin D_3. Have your doctor do a blood test to check your vitamin levels before starting a supplement regimen.

Look into light therapy

Getting enough light is beneficial for mental well being, especially if you live in a part of the world where there are few hours of sunlight. Find ways to get the maximum amount of light into your home. Put in skylights, use white or light-colored paint, and keep the blinds open during the day. Swap out your light bulbs for ones that mimic daylight. You can also purchase the type of light box that doctors recommend for light therapy (sunbox.com has great ones).

Use hydrotherapy

Doing water aerobics, sitting in a hot tub, using a steam room, soaking your feet, or simply taking a hot bath or shower can all help you relax and lift your mood.

Get plenty of exercise

Doing some form of physical exercise regularly is essential. Exercising at a gym or at home, taking yoga classes, or even just going for walks can be a natural antidepressant and mood-booster. It's even better if you can exercise outdoors and have the added benefits of fresh air and being in nature.

Try touch therapy

Massage has some of the same benefits as exercise, releasing endorphins that reduce stress. A pedicure or facial can be as relaxing, whether at home or at a spa.

Do something creative or hands-on

Creative activities like writing and painting are relaxing and can help us be in the present moment. They also help us deal with uncertainty.

Professional artist and Dirty Footprints Studio founder Connie Solera writes on her blog about how she deals with uncertainty: she paints like mad! This creative release grounds her when she's feeling overwhelmed, and lets her mind relax into bringing her the answers she's looking for. Painting brings Connie into alignment with herself and gives her a deeper knowing of what step she should take next. She says she also spends time in nature every day because it grounds and centers her in a similar way.

Have a healthy mindset

When my daughter was sixteen, she shared this advice for staying healthy: look for the positives all around you. She'd gone through quite a few moves by then, and she admitted that sometimes it's very difficult to prevent yourself from getting stressed or depressed. But she's found that the best way for her to handle this has been to find the positives. She suggests, for instance, finding a park, museum, or even just a street you like and walking around it often. This is a great way to start making emotional connections to your location.

Using Mindfulness

If we can adjust our mindset to be mindful and present, we have a much higher chance of being happy. Step five of Maripat Abbot's relocation process for executives and their families is about being more mindful. She says that "going from one home to another" or "straddling two zip codes," is when accidents happen the most. There's a lot on the mind and too much to do, and it's not uncommon for people to have minor car accidents and falls, all because they aren't fully present in the current moment. She says, "You are not in your feet, not in your breath, not touching the earth, so to speak."

Eat mindfully

Abbott also reminds people to eat mindfully. When we're mindful, we're more likely to nourish our body by thinking about what we put into it and how certain foods make us feel. When we're rushing around and not really in the present moment, we're more likely to eat comfort foods and gain extra pounds. (I call them my moving pounds, only I can't move them!)

Keep a list of healthy restaurants handy. Try to find easy-to-cook or pre-prepared healthy meals, or cook in bulk and freeze for those days when you're too tired or sick. Get the whole family together for a night of cooking and you could have quick, easy frozen meals for weeks!

Accessing the Safety and Security within Us

When we're surrounded by chaos, it's important to ground ourselves and create inner harmony. Everyone does this differently—I do it through writing, listening to music, and meditating. I especially love Deepak Chopra and Oprah Winfrey's twenty-one-day meditation series that they offer from time to time on chopracentermeditation.com. It's even free!

Chopra shows us how we can access our own inner sense of security when everything around us is chaotic. On day one of the twenty-one-day series about finding security, he provides us with this affirmation: "My peace and security are within me." Then he teaches us how to awaken the flow of security in us. He says, "Everyone has the basic need to feel safe. Without it, life feels insecure and stress magnifies that insecurity."

He goes on to say, "We also have a core of stability inside that we can return to throughout the ups and downs of everyday life. Once you experience this safe place inside, you have found the flow of security, the core of yourself that isn't shaken by outer events. Centered in this place, you can access a space of safety and security, even when you're having a bad day or facing a personal challenge."

It's comforting to know that in the midst of feeling unsafe and insecure, we have the power to ground ourselves with feelings of safety, security, stability, and peace.

Love Circles

I think of circles
When I think of love,
Not hearts.
Like ripples in a pond,
Ever-increasing
As each stone skips along.

There's comfort
In the encircling embrace
Of a loved one
And promise of eternity
In a ring.

Wholesome,
The love of family
To make you feel complete.
Each generation apart,
Yet a part of
The Great Circle
Connected by love.

Kiran Prasad

Chapter 7

Love and Belonging

There are no strangers here, only friends you haven't met yet.
WILLIAM BUTLER YEATS

In *Daring Greatly*, research professor Brené Brown writes, "We are hardwired for connection—it's what gives purpose and meaning to our lives. The absence of love, belonging, and connection always leads to suffering."

I've known such suffering well. The loneliness of the early months in a foreign city is soul-crushing! I ached to connect and belong. As Irish poet and philosopher John O'Donohue writes in *Eternal Echoes: Celtic Reflections on Our Yearning to Belong*, "Our hunger to belong is the longing to find a bridge across the distance from isolation to intimacy. Everyone longs for intimacy and dreams of a nest of belonging in which one is embraced, seen, and loved."

According to most people I interviewed, the desire for love, connection, and intimacy is one of the hardest needs to satisfy. It's what makes us search for a tribe of like-minded individuals to accept us for who we are. Our family is usually the first group we turn to.

Staying Close as a Family

Without local friends to share our joys and fears with at first, we can end up venting to—and taking our frustrations out on—those closest to us. This happened to my family when we moved to Oregon, but we also spent more quality time together as we explored what the area had to offer. (In Portland, this was hiking, biking, and eating at wonderful restaurants.) A move can bring a family together or tear it apart.

Connect daily

Whenever we were at home, I insisted on all of us eating together at the dining table, without the distraction of TV and other electronics. We had a tradition of playing a game I devised, called "What made you mad, glad, or sad?" This involved going around the table and saying what made us happy, angry, or sad that day. If nothing made a person happy, we had to tell that person a joke or find something to make them laugh. It helped us connect daily and tune in to our children's emotions about the move.

Communicating with teens

When my kids became teenagers, their endless chatter turned to monosyllabic replies, which meant I had to change my strategy. On our drives home from school, I found that if I gave them space and asked nothing, they usually told me about their day. Staying quiet was a challenge for me, because I prefer speaking to listening! A book I've found helpful to improve communication with children is *How to Talk so Kids Will Listen & Listen so Kids Will Talk*, by Adele Faber and Elaine Mazlish. Although their advice is geared toward younger children, it could work with teens, too.

A 2014 article on the Better Health Channel, "Teenagers and Communication," has this tip for improving interactions with teenagers: "Remember that we are all given two ears and one mouth. This is to remind us that we should spend twice as much time listening as talking. This is especially important when talking to teenagers, who may tell us more if we are silent long enough to give them the opportunity."

It's challenging to get the attention of teenagers. They can become distant, moody, even angry and depressed. In an effort to belong, they might spend more time with friends or on activities (including online ones). As teens, my kids would blame me for turning their lives upside down, even though the decision to relocate was their father's!

Be supportive

Although they misdirected their resentment at me, I tried to understand and be supportive. One of the ways I did this was by showing affection. In his book *The Five Love Languages*, Gary Chapman helps us determine what someone's ideal type of affection might be. The five love languages are gifts, quality time, words of affirmation, acts of service, and physical touch. Physical affection is important for everyone, especially kids. It lets them know that the caregiver or parent is still there, that there's at least one constant in the moving equation.

Teenagers in particular aren't always willing to admit they need affection. When my children were teenagers and acted as though they were too old for hugs, I told them it was *me* who needed the hugs (which I usually do!). Showing affection is a great way to connect with loved ones (including pets!).

While I provided support to my family, I usually found myself with none. Families are meant to be a team and be there for one another, but family members aren't always physically or emotionally available. A spouse or partner can be away on business a lot or emotionally not present because of the stress of a new job (as was the case for me). This can strain relationships.

Maintaining Intimate Relationships

Intimate relationships can suffer under all the tremendous change that relocation brings. If left unchecked, this can lead to a breakup or divorce. Robin Pascoe's book, *A Moveable Marriage*, has wonderful advice on how to relocate a relationship without breaking it. She explains, "Like any new home, a moveable marriage may require a few renovations to make it comfortable to live in. *A marriage isn't like water.* It doesn't pour neatly into whatever vessel is set out to contain it. A few metaphorical walls may need to be knocked down and put back up again, in a different place. The contractors for the job are you and your husband."

Stay in love from afar

Close relationships can suffer even if loved ones aren't relocating together. Zane, who was still attending college in California when his girlfriend Nadine got a job in another city, says it takes constant "tuning"; little adjustments you have to make as you learn more about each other's needs. When they were first apart, he noticed how much of a presence she had been in his life. Nadine missed "losing that sense of comfort and this person you can instantly turn to—that instant understanding. Having that much of a feeling of belonging to someone, you don't want to give that up just because of your physical location." They scheduled regular trips to see each other, which was key to their success.

Vijay and Vanessa did the same when Vijay moved back to his hometown in England. Vijay's advice is to set aside time every day for quality communication. He said that although it's great to have many modes of connecting with each other, it also has its negatives: not communicating fast enough is frowned upon and not getting back to someone at all is not tolerated, for instance. He prefers face-to-face communication and feels that virtual interaction, like texting and emailing, has its problems. Messages can be misunderstood.

Although they're managing their long-distance relationship well, neither Vijay nor Vanessa would recommend it to others.

Connecting Virtually

These days, many of us feel lonely and disconnected. Like Vijay, we prefer face-to-face interactions, yet we spend more time connecting virtually. In an article for expatexpert.com titled "Culture Shock in the Digital World," Robin Pascoe advises that in the early stages of transition (and if used to connect with local people), these virtual connections provide a lifeline, and have a major impact on the traditional stages of culture shock. But if used globally, she says, they can "delay the process of working through these stages." This is because, she explains, virtual connection is not real interaction, and it may cause us to "falsely feel rooted in communities that are not nearby" and keep us in a "dreamlike state."

After relocating to Portland, I experienced this dreamlike state. I continued working remotely as a secretary for a cultural organization, even helping edit their directory. I'd played an active role in this organization (to an extent that I found it painful to see pictures online of the wonderful events they continued to organize without me). I was in denial about my reality, and I didn't have a role in my new community yet.

Connecting Locally

Volunteer in your community

It's not always possible to find paid work right away, and volunteering can fill those empty hours, take our minds off things, and connect us to others. A 2001 study by Peggy Thoits and Lyndi Hewitt called "Volunteer Work and Well-Being" showed that the happiest people tend to be those who are more involved with their communities, especially through volunteer work. Community engagement can get people through difficult times, while a lack of human interaction, relationships, or sense of belonging can lead to depression and loneliness.

Pamela, a community-minded mother of two, says the one thing that really helped her establish social contacts was to jump in and help an organization. She attended a parent–teacher association (PTA) meeting before she even had her boxes unpacked! She found that volunteering right away, even though it was the worst time in her life to give away time, helped her form the most lasting relationships.

Integrating into a Foreign Culture

Communities, and cultures within them, vary greatly. Simon, an English as a Second Language (ESL) teacher is no stranger to this. He worked in Kazakhstan and Macedonia with the Peace Corps. He taught in South Korea and China too.

Coworkers always ask him what his secret is; how he's able to transition well. He tells them that he goes to countries with no expectations, because the more expectations you have, the narrower your vision. One suggestion he has for adapting to another culture is to behave as a guest in a person's home and try to put yourself in their shoes. That way you're far less likely to be critical and judgmental.

Know the customs and etiquette

Until we learn the customs and etiquette of a foreign culture, it's difficult to know how to present ourselves to others. We wonder if there's a dress code at social functions, what we should bring to parties, and how to greet one another. We worry about how friendly people are, which topics of conversation are socially acceptable, and what the political beliefs are. Before we become familiar with all this, it's a source of stress.

Celebrate new holidays

We can feel like outsiders looking in until we do things like celebrate holidays as the locals do. When we first moved to America, Halloween, Thanksgiving, and the Fourth of July were foreign concepts to us. Then some wonderful friends included us in celebrating them.

The Kendonsky family took us to a farm for Halloween and helped our children pick out and carve pumpkins. They also shared the fall tradition of apple picking with us, and afterward we got to enjoy the treat of donuts and freshly pressed apple cider. I can still smell it! At Thanksgiving, the Sharma family helped us feel at home. Through them, we learned to embrace the foods that are typically eaten on this holiday, and my daughter developed a love for pumpkin pie! Every Fourth of July, the Sandler family invited us to their annual barbecue. It was fun being patriotic and wearing clothes to match the theme (even though our British friends joked about it being an anti-British holiday).

By celebrating these holidays, my family started to feel less like outsiders. We can really benefit from the diversity we're exposed to if we open ourselves up to it.

Gain from diversity

After moving to California with her boyfriend, Katherine found herself in a city with greater ethnic diversity: for the first time, she was in the minority. This wasn't something she was used to, but she adjusted by taking up new interests. She learned to make sushi, joined a pottery class, and began to gain from the multi-ethnic culture of her location.

Learn about work culture

Mark, our frequent mover, says he faced a change in work culture, most notably in the difference between the English and American work ethic. Mark's friend (who lives in America) warned him that he would spend more time in meetings. In England, Mark was used to doing things first and *then* talking about them. The change in work culture was challenging for the first few months, until Mark started thinking like the locals and doing things the way they did.

Get cultural support

If you're working outside the home, you might have an employee relocation specialist helping you navigate the changes in corporate culture. Schools and colleges could benefit from such a person too—schools usually offer a small amount of relocation support on student orientation day, but ideally this would extend well beyond a single day. Incoming students need continuous help throughout the first few weeks and months.

Parents who don't work outside the home could benefit from cultural assistance as well. Too often, companies that transfer an employee leave their accompanying partner without support. I experienced this when we arrived in America. My husband's company transferred in over six hundred expats from around the world, yet it made no effort to connect us with one another. I felt isolated when I could have had the support of others going through the same thing. One company I know of has monthly coffee mornings for accompanying spouses, led by a cultural coordinator. Now that's a company with a heart!

Years after we relocated to the U.S., I appreciated it when my children's high school held a coffee morning and orientation for parents. It helped me connect with the school culture and become familiar with the layout. One school even offered, "mentor families" to help in those early months. I wish more schools—and companies—offered this type of assistance.

Dealing with daily cultural differences is draining. One woman told me she felt like she'd moved to Mars! When everything else has changed, it's understandable to gravitate toward something familiar by turning to our roots. Expats often turn to their culture or become more patriotic about their country of origin the longer they've been away from it.

I found myself doing this when I joined an Indian cultural organization—I even ended up on the board. Then, when I moved to Oregon, I joined a British expat group. Our cultures are part of who we are: just as we reassemble our furniture after a move, we try to reassemble the pieces of our identity.

After being uprooted, connecting to our cultural heritage can help us find our feet, as Sunaina, the young bride who relocated to England, discovered. She was having a difficult transition when I checked in with her during the first months. Then she followed my advice and joined a number of Meetups (which I'll explain later). She got to know women from those groups, and now runs a seventy-six-member expat Meetup for American wives! In just a few months, everything changed.

Although it's great at first to seek support from our culture of origin, try not to become dependent on it or restrict yourself to it. Connecting with people from other backgrounds is enriching. Jazz, the Indian student who relocated to Canada, tells me that he didn't seek out Indian friends. He feels very strongly about this, saying that if you move abroad and only try to find others from your country, you're basically not moving—it's like coming to Canada while still trying to be in India.

Facing Language Differences

If you're in a foreign country, it will be harder to learn the language if you isolate yourself from the host culture. When I was tutoring an English as a Second Language (ESL) student from China, her mother asked me how she could improve her own English. One of my biggest pieces of advice to her was to immerse herself in the English language instead of restricting herself to the Chinese language. Schools often use the immersion method because they believe it helps students learn a language faster.

Language differences—including the accent, dialect, or vocabulary—can be a barrier to getting to know the culture and people in a foreign city. My family found that variations between British and American English could cause confusion. When my daughter was a toddler, she said to her preschool teacher, "Nappy, nappy," trying to convey that she needed a diaper change ("nappy" means diaper in England). Instead, her teacher told her to take a nap! As for me, with my strong British accent, I had trouble doing simple tasks like ordering food at the deli. At first, I resisted modifying my accent or vocabulary. After a while of being misunderstood, I reluctantly gave in.

Language and humor

Understanding the jokes and sense of humor is another issue that expats face. Sunaina says, "I never realized how awful it feels to constantly be the person in the room who doesn't get a reference or a joke. The sense of humor is different here. There are new holidays, expressions, and sensibilities for me to grasp. It will take time."

I empathize with her; it took me a while to follow jokes in the U.S. Americans didn't understand my humor and I didn't get theirs.

Meeting People and Making Friends

Be the initiator

Whether you face a foreign language or not, in order to make friends, *you* have to be the initiator. You need a friend more than the other person; therefore, you have to take the first step.

Use body language

Think of someone who's really approachable. What makes them this way? Some of us are naturally good at using body language, while others need to learn this valuable skill.

The easiest way to break the ice is to use open-armed gestures and smile, even if no one smiles at you first. It's worth the wrinkles! Also, show interest in the other person by making eye contact.

Know the culture first to avoid sending wrong signals, as I did at my local gym. In my previous town, smiling at everyone—including strangers of the opposite sex—was the norm. Apparently, in this town it wasn't and could be mistaken for flirtation!

Go out

To make friends, you have to go out—you certainly won't meet anyone if you hibernate at home, are too busy to socialize, or spend all your time renovating your house. Make time: accept invites and opportunities, even if they seem unappealing at first. It's especially important to go out daily if you don't work outside the home. Those initial months as a newcomer can be extremely lonely if no one knows you exist. Therefore, get yourself known.

Talk to strangers

It's important to get used to going up to complete strangers and talking to them. Obviously, make sure you're in a safe, public place. Talk to people wherever you go, whether it's out walking the dog, at the doctor's office, at the gym, or at school or work events. Inform everyone you meet that you're new in town. Often, I would strike up a conversation by asking about the neighborhood or where I could buy particular items—people love to help. Other times I would give someone a compliment about their accent or hairstyle (and ask who their stylist was!). People are extremely receptive when you show interest in them or their neighborhood.

Make friends even if you're shy

Those who know me may be surprised to hear that I'm naturally shy. Although approaching strangers is difficult for me, I still push myself to do it. If you're too shy to approach strangers, consider the people who provide you with services as potential friends. An acquaintance of mine still has close ties to her banking broker, tax person, and their families. Another option is to make friends through online interest groups.

Always get a contact number

The art of making friends is similar to dating, I've been told: you have to be proactive even though it might be uncomfortable, and you have to exchange numbers at the end of the meeting because you might never see them again. Many of us may be afraid of doing this for fear of rejection. It's not easy to pluck up the courage to ask for contact information, but it's essential you do. Some homeowner associations make this easier by having a residents' directory. I found it extremely useful! It's becoming common for schools to have directories too.

While most of us use an address book or cell phone to exchange information, Jill, an administrative assistant, uses calling cards. The cards feature her last name printed at the top, with all the family members' names listed below. The cards include her family's street address, phone numbers, and email addresses. She finds it far easier to hand someone a card than to go looking for a pen and paper to exchange numbers. Calling cards are a great tool for personal networking.

Do some networking

There are various ways to build personal networks. During my first month in Oregon, I was determined to speak to at least two people a day. Try not to be picky about who you meet at first. Even if you don't have a lot in common with someone, they can introduce you to someone you do connect with.

Once, an acquaintance invited me to a coffee morning for spouses of another company's employees. Despite the fact that I wasn't affiliated with that company and was already feeling alienated, I agreed to go because it was a chance to meet people. To my surprise, I found it easy to interact with those women because they were fellow expats. Before leaving, I collected the email addresses of the women I enjoyed talking to and sent them a group message so we could all stay in touch.

Connect in the workplace

My husband tells me that the main way he makes friends in the workplace is by talking to colleagues about things he's interested in. That way, people with similar interests gravitate toward him. Eventually he gets to know a few of them better, either at lunch or while traveling, and he builds on those initial bonds.

In addition to doing what her dad does, my daughter also seeks out people at work who have an attitude she admires or a value system that matches hers. For instance, people who love travel, or are open-minded and family-oriented. Then she establishes routines with those acquaintances, like going to the gym, to build the relationships. It's not always easy to find a niche we can fit into.

Finding a Niche

Find the right kind of people

When I moved to Indiana, I invited a few ladies over for coffee only to feel dejected afterward because my efforts at friendship were in vain. These people didn't need friends as much as I did because they had extended family close by. Nina, a new friend, suggested that I'd met the wrong kind of people and that she would introduce me to the right kind. With her help, I eventually made friends I was compatible with.

Annika, who faced frequent moves because her father was in the military, says her most challenging time was when she was fifteen. It was after relocating from the Philippines, where she felt she really belonged, to America. She says it wasn't easy getting to know students who'd grown up together and who didn't have a military background. She found herself, now in tenth grade, having to start all over again. Trying to fit into the little cliques was difficult.

Certain individuals are simply wrong for us as friends when we're newcomers. Residents who dislike the place we've moved to, for instance, are likely to spread their negativity to us. Maya experienced this when she moved to California for college. She lived in a dorm with some students who hated dorm life. My brother had a similar experience when he moved to Canada; a few of his new friends were disillusioned with the place and seemed to only highlight the negative aspects of living there. I know at the start of a move we can't be too picky about friends, but later we should seek opportunities and people who raise our spirits rather than bring us down.

Make different friends for different needs

Don't expect one friend to fulfill all your friendship needs. I have friends who I specifically go on walks with, or see movies with, or have dinner parties with. I have writer friends, spiritual friends, and book club friends, too.

This means you'll have to stop thinking about friendship simply in terms of compatibility of age, intellectual background, or one of the other boxes we put people into. I have friends of all ages, nationalities, and backgrounds. It opens you up to more friendships, as long as it's someone who needs a friend and has at least one thing in common.

Join social/interest groups

Joining a social or interest-based group will help you meet like-minded people. Sarah, of Oregon, has been through many international moves. After she figured out why she'd been miserable in Kenya (she hadn't found a niche), she joined twenty clubs at her university in Northern Ireland. She says that those groups were invaluable to her; she only wishes they existed for everyone, not just first-year students at college.

Actually, there is something like that everywhere! Meetup is an international organization of local interest groups: when you discover it, you'll only wish you'd found it sooner. From anywhere in the world, you can type in your zip code on the meetup.com website and search for Meetups for diverse interests such as hiking, reading, witchcraft, salsa dancing, pug ownership, and amateur philosophy.

If a group you're interested in doesn't exist, Meetup has a simple system to help you create one. You can connect face to face at monthly Meetups across your city as well as online. I recommend it so often that anyone would think I have shares in the company!

Getting Local Support through Clubs

Get support for newcomers

If family members aren't able to support us, we have to turn to others. When someone passes away, help and sympathy are offered to the bereaved. Similarly, there needs to be a support system for people facing the losses of relocation. The early months are when we need it most, as we don't have any local friends.

A neighborhood can give that support through caring neighbors or community members. Organizations like the Newcomers Club provide this welcome nationally and internationally. There are even groups specific to a particular need, such as spousal support, or a specific culture, like the British Women's Club, which is available in many international locations.

I've had good and bad experiences in these types of groups. Don't give up if one group doesn't work out; there will be others better suited to your needs.

Whichever group you decide to join, try to be honest about what you're feeling. In my experience, people are very helpful once they know what you're going through. Jane, a lady I met at a dog park, was extremely empathic toward me during a tough week after my move to Oregon. She took me out for lunch and gave me a tour of the neighborhood. I couldn't believe how kind she was, and I still call her "my little angel." She rescued me when I most needed it because I opened up to her.

Find spiritual connection

Joining a local church or having spiritual connectedness could brighten your first months. I never felt the need for religious or spiritual support until recently, when I went through a difficult period in my life. It led me on a quest to find peace through self-help, positive psychology, and spirituality books. I finally found a local center for spirituality that ties in with my beliefs, and for the first time in my life, I feel I belong. It's because I'm among others who think as I do and share the same values. I've found my spiritual home!

It's a strange coincidence that as I was writing this chapter on belonging, I attended a service at my center called "Yearning to Belong." During that service, Reverend Kathleen McKern Verigin asked us to look inside ourselves for what is causing separation. She says that when we do that, we stop feeling the isolation. We see the oneness in the universe and realize, *I belong to me*. We are in dire need of this unity-minded consciousness these days, when there's a sense of division in the world.

If you need religious guidance based on Christian principles, I can strongly recommend Susan Miller's book, *After the Boxes Are Unpacked*. It's a wonderful resource, as is her website (susanmiller.org). She also provides support for newcomers in churches nationwide.

Get online support

If you're unable to travel to connect with others due to health or other constraints, you can get online support. There are usually plenty of forums and teleconferences available to people in these situations. I had to depend on this kind of support when I became sick and housebound. It's important to connect with others when you're depressed or in pain. That's when you need it most.

Using Your Tribal Instinct

If you can't find a group to belong to, you can create your own by bringing together all the people you meet, as Sunaina did with the American wives she met at Meetups. True friendships come from being there for one another, and friends really can become family in the absence of real family. Forming our own groups allows us to remain true to ourselves, since we don't have to conform to other people's expectations of us.

I've always struggled to belong. When I started attending my local center for spirituality, I finally found somewhere I could truly be myself and be understood by others. My wish for you is that you'll also find that kind of connection and belong again.

Who am I?

I Google my name . . .
I find doctors, scientists,
Actors, award winners.
But where the homemaker,
Mother and wife?
For that
There are no accolades.

Kiran Prasad

Chapter 8

Esteem

The worst loneliness is to not be comfortable with yourself.

MARK TWAIN

Maslow believed esteem could come from others as well as ourselves; that in order to feel it, we need to be loved, accepted, and recognized for our capabilities. In *Motivation and Personality*, he explains how, once we have a certain amount of confidence and self-esteem, we're more able to be creative, to grow, and to use our talents to serve others.

Spiritual leaders such as Wayne Dyer and Deepak Chopra believe true self-esteem doesn't come from others or anything outside of us; it comes from within. We'll explore this idea later. For now, we'll focus on Maslow's view of how self-worth can come from others' perceptions of us.

Achieving Your Goals

Relocating can impact self-worth, and it especially affects children when they transition from one grade to the next and one town to another. In their previous school, they might be known for being really smart or good at a sport, only to lose that reputation with a move. The effects of mobility on student achievement have been well recorded.

A 2009 review of sixteen studies, titled "School Mobility and Educational Success," shows that children who relocated three or more times dropped out of school at a higher rate than those who had more stability. Two of the studies, in Baltimore and Chicago, show a decrease in standardized test scores for every move a child makes.

Basically, this research shows that mobility has a negative effect on achievement, which worsens with every move. The transition to junior high, or middle school as we now call it (ages eleven to fifteen, approximately), was found to be the most challenging for many kids. It doesn't surprise me; I've taught at middle schools and know how those years are already the most difficult for students.

When we lived in Michigan and my husband accepted a job in Indiana, my children and I stayed behind for a year to let my son finish middle school. During that time, I completed my Master's degree. When I finally had the certification in my hands, I felt a huge sense of achievement. My son also appreciated being able to stay at one school for its entire range of grades. In the light of these findings on student achievement, I'm glad we didn't disrupt his schooling during those years!

In her 2008 article on Oprah.com, "Groundbreaking Research on Self-Esteem," Aimee Lee Ball writes that the nineties was the era of self-esteem, when we believed we could raise children's self-esteem simply by making them feel good about themselves despite any actual accomplishments. She goes on to point out that recently, these ideas have been turned around by studies such as those of Stanford University psychology professor Carol Dweck. Her studies show that instead of praising a child, it's more effective to praise the *process the child has been through*—the effort, strategy, perseverance, or improvement.

Dweck says the idea that self-esteem can be handed to children on a plate is a harmful one. Parents think they're helping their kids, when really they're making them less resilient. What's more helpful is to teach them life skills such as empathy, decision-making, relationship building, and stress management.

These skills are great for adults to develop, too. Psychologist Daniel Goleman writes about these in his best-selling book, *Emotional Intelligence*. According to Goleman, self-esteem is "a realistic assessment of your strengths and weaknesses." It can be better thought of as self-mastery.

Mastering What You Love

A move affects our ability to reach a level of mastery in something. This is because staying in one location for some time provides the stability needed to excel. In my son's case, he was progressing well in Boy Scouts and wanted to become an Eagle Scout, the highest level of scouting. At his next school, he knew no one in the local Boy Scout program, which made it uncomfortable due to all the camping and teamwork required. The program was run very differently and consequently, he didn't continue with it. Often, the extracurricular activities my children loved were totally different from their previous school's offerings or not available at all.

As for me, I wasn't able to reach the level of mastery that I aspired to in my profession. I wanted to go on to do a Ph.D. at the university where I did my Master's and teach there as a professor, but moving interfered with that plan. This happened with a few of my personal interests, too. I had an excellent piano teacher and voice coach in Michigan and was making great progress, but I couldn't find suitable replacements in Indiana. Also, I became too busy settling in and remodeling the next house again. It's frustrating to have to keep giving up things you love.

Staying Independent

Our sense of independence can be impacted after relocating. One way in which we lose our independence is when we physically struggle to navigate our way around an unfamiliar city or neighborhood on our own. This happened to me when we first moved to America and I was too scared to drive in a new country.

A newcomer becomes dependent in many ways. It's hard to accept, especially if you're independent-minded. Although men are increasingly moving for their partner's career, it's still mostly women who are the accompanying partner. They can become dependent if they can't find work, especially if they were previously employed. Anne Gillmé, founder of the Expatriate Connection, an online resource for expats, especially accompanying spouses, knows this firsthand. In a 2015 interview with vocation-village.com's Janet Civitelli ("How to Survive Culture Shock when Moving for a New Job"), Anne explains a few of the challenges that accompanying spouses face. "In some cases, they don't have the opportunity to find another professional activity because they lack a work permit/visa or recognition of their professional qualifications. In other cases, they have to find work, a highly demanding task in the current troubled economic situation. The lack of professional activity is often a deal breaker in the morale of the accompanying partner leading to loss of self-confidence, loss of self-esteem, and financial dependence."

A number of times, I had to give up a job and had difficulty getting another one, or at least at the same level as a previous one. As a teacher, I was required to recertify in some of the U.S. states I moved to. Job-hunting was disheartening, especially during tough economic times. As a newcomer, it was even tougher because I didn't have a network of people who could refer me for positions. Reluctantly, I would return to the role of homemaker, having to repeatedly become dependent on my husband.

Preventing Being Dominated

In the workplace, at school, or even in the community, newcomers are easily dominated. New kids in particular are easy targets for bullying. This is something parents should watch out for, especially in the early months after a relocation.

Social domination can occur in any environment, but research by psychologists Anthony Pellegrini and Maria Bartini suggests that bullying begins in elementary school and gets worse during the transitions from elementary to middle school and from middle to high school.

I've seen bullying firsthand as a teacher, especially in middle school. Having relocated often as a child, I've experienced it personally as well. New students are vulnerable to being dominated because bullies tend to pick on socially isolated kids with no friends to defend them. They also target people who find it hard to fit in because of how they dress, speak, or behave. Without friends, new kids can turn to online activities and become vulnerable to cyber bullying.

School staff, parents, and caregivers need to be extra vigilant, especially in those early months after a move. They need to recognize warning signs: changes in behavior and health such as sleep, appetite, frequent stomachaches and headaches, or not wanting to go to school. They can also help children make friends quicker by encouraging them to enroll in clubs, groups, and activities. To learn more, go to stopbullying.gov. Bullying must be prevented; it can really affect a child's self-esteem.

Acquiring Status and Prestige

In an individualistic society like the U.S., self-esteem comes mostly from our work status. A work-related move often leads to a rise in status or prestige for one partner and a lowering for the other. This can be difficult to accept, especially if you've built a name for yourself. Promotions typically go to people who are well established and have proven their worth. To receive anywhere near the same level of recognition that we once had, we have to wait patiently until we're established again.

If you've moved frequently as I have, you'll know that maintaining a career isn't easy. Ideally, accompanying partners would have what Jo Parfitt calls a "portable career." Jo, the founder of Summertime Publishing, specializes in inspiring others to write about expatriate issues. She co-wrote *A Career in Your Suitcase*, and explained to me in an email that "a portable career is one that moves when you do, is based on what you most love to do, and gives your life meaning. It may not be paid work, it can just as easily be volunteer work or study or a portfolio of different elements. The word career comes from the French and actually just means a 'journey.'"

She went on to say that a portable career isn't something you do briefly to kill time and then give up when you move to the next place. If it's the right job, it will grow and enrich you over time and from posting to posting. Jo is a great role model for this because her own portable career has brought her much happiness. Now she's excited to say that she's providing other accompanying partners with a career model that's completely mobile. You can find out more at careerinyoursuitcase.com.

Robin Pascoe has similarly redefined a career as "a path through life," not simply a professional vocation. In an online interview with Career by Choice founder Megan Fitzgerald, Pascoe informs us that when a career is seen in this way, especially by women, it allows them to incorporate what's important to them, whether it's raising children, volunteering in their communities, being a homemaker, or traveling to amazing places. It allows a person to be judged not by what they do but who they are.

I wish I'd discovered this sooner instead of seeing my career simply as a profession dependent on whether someone recognized my teaching qualifications from state to state. Well it's never too late to redefine our path in life! It's what I'm trying to do now.

Gaining Respect from Others

Titles and labels

We may have built up a certain level of respect from people in our workplace or community, which we lose after relocating. We may also lose many of the labels that contributed to our identity, and struggle to find ones to replace them. For instance, when our kids grow up and leave home, as primary caregivers we somewhat lose our parenting title and role. We become "empty nesters," which emphasizes loss. What if we replaced that label with one that signifies renewal and growth? A more positive and respectful title would be "veteran parent." I much prefer that!

In Indiana, I was well respected and known in the community as the secretary of a cultural organization. I lost that after moving. In fact, I became anonymous, or "just a housewife." A housewife or homemaker is much more than this of course, yet Western society gives this choice of vocation little recognition or status. It's no wonder that these days many women feel ashamed to associate with this label.

In the same email conversation, Jo Parfitt wrote, "I realized that, for me, I was not prepared to be 'just a something.' Many accompanying partners say they are 'just a housewife' when you ask them what they do, and then they give a weak laugh and look at the floor. I didn't want that. I wanted people to ask me what I did for a living and not just assume that I spent my days at the beauty parlor or tennis court. In short, I wanted a label. I wanted a professional identity."

She explained that she wanted this not to stand out or be different, but because until she became an expat wife, it was normal for her to be working. In Dubai, newly married at age twenty-six, she had nothing to do, nothing of interest to her. She'd lost herself. Finally, over time, she found things that were a good fit. A year later, she was doing freelance writing and running a computer-training department and résumé service. She found her tribe and found a label. Jo's story is inspiring. Today, six moves and twenty-eight years later, she's a writer, publisher, and teacher.

Find your true self

Wayne Dyer offers another perspective on the labels that contribute to our identity. In his book *You'll See It When You Believe It*, he writes at great length about how we become too attached to our labels and why it's healthier to let them go. He says that when we don't focus on labels or titles to define us, we get to the essence of who we are: our authentic self.

He believes, as does Deepak Chopra, that titles, awards, and accolades are not real. We can be stripped of them at any time. Dyer and Chopra's message is that if we focus more on being our authentic self, rather than on how others define us, we might feel better about ourselves. This perspective really helps when our self-esteem and sense of identity are shaken up after relocating.

Gaining Self-Respect

Maintain your self-identity

Depending on your stage in life, relocation can have a huge impact on self-identity. My frequent moves, especially at midlife, left me reevaluating who I am and where I'd like my life to go (not unlike what my children were going through in adolescence!) This is because, as with any major change, relocation affects your whole being: your personality, values, and belief systems. It can shake the core foundation of who you think you are. You might find you don't want to attend church anymore, or become cynical about relationships or dissatisfied with your choice of career. Whatever it is, there's usually some shift in thinking.

Reassemble yourself

This shift in thinking can make it difficult to reassemble the pieces of our identity after relocating, as aspects of who we are may no longer fit into our new life. As William Bridges writes in *Transitions: Making Sense of Life's Changes:* "No longer being . . . wife or a salesman, no longer being the old me or a young person is a source of panic. That is when it is important to remember the significance of disidentification and the need to lessen the bonds of who we think we are so that we can go through a transition toward a new identity."

What Bridges is saying is that if we can no longer identify with our previous self, with who we thought we were, it's best to loosen ties with that identity. Perhaps our true self is hidden underneath the superficial layer of what others tell us we are. In the words of Lao Tzu, poet and philosopher of ancient China, "When I let go of what I am, I become what I might be."

Start with a clean slate

For some, a fresh identity comes from leaving emotional baggage behind and starting over. Unfortunately, if we don't put in the time to leave well, our baggage will follow. We can reinvent ourselves somewhat (Annika, who moved frequently due to her father's military career, even changed her name), but we still take our ingrained patterns of behavior with us.

Portland, Oregon, where I currently live, has been a great place to reinvent myself as a writer. The dark, rainy days that keep me indoors are the perfect environment for creative endeavors. It's not surprising we have a large literary population here, as well as musicians and artists.

Although I complain about the rain quite a lot, I should be thankful because it's helping me become an author!

I've come to appreciate how every city I've lived in has given me something; they've each added another layer to who I am. It seems like moving allows us to shed one skin of identity and/or grow another. This might explain why certain people love to relocate! Although benefits can be gleaned from being able to start afresh, we must make sure we don't rely on this repeatedly so as to avoid having to be ourselves.

Accept yourself

Frequent moving has been referred to as "pulling a geographic" by some therapists. It's an expression used by Alcoholics Anonymous (AA) to describe people who search for "external changes to change internal problems," as Sarah Kershaw explains in her 2010 *New York Times* article, "The Psychology of Moving." When life becomes unmanageable, they relocate in the false belief that it will fix their problems. They blame things outside of themselves instead of looking inside, where the problem really lies.

In the same article, Kershaw speaks with psychologist Elizabeth Stirling, who specializes in helping people with difficult transitions. Stirling tells us, "No matter how much you move, you still take yourself with you."

Reverend Noel McInnis, whom I had the pleasure of working with in a writing group, opens his public presentations with the words:

Everywhere I go, here I am
Everywhere I go, here I am,
No matter where or when

I may go, just then,
Wherever I show up, here I am.

He sang this to us with his guitar. When I asked him to explain the lyrics, he told me that thirty years ago, he wondered if God had a theme song, and what that might be. Immediately, these words came to him with an accompanying melody.

Uncover your true nature

If we can't completely leave our true self behind, we may as well embrace it. Endings, as explained earlier, lead to the in-between or neutral zone of Bridges' transition model. This neutral zone can be a great time for self-reflection and introversion, if we allow it to be. If channeled in the right way, it may even help us become our true self.

Grow and be transformed

Personal growth happens most when we're shaken out of the familiar and into unfamiliar territory, especially when this is accompanied by deep suffering. As Wayne Muller, author of *How Then, Shall We Live?*, puts it, "When we come close to those things that break us down, we touch those things that also break us open. And in that breaking open, we uncover our true nature." Just as a chrysalis emerges into a beautiful butterfly, we can emerge as the person we were always meant to be.

Maureen, a military wife who has moved often, explains to me how every single place she's lived in becomes part of her personality as she adapts to it and grows from it. She says, "When I'm transplanted somewhere else, my roots take a beating, and it hurts. Every move, even from one house to another house in the same area, can be a trauma to my system."

This reminds me of a well-known quote by writer and journalist Anatole France: "All changes, even the most longed for, have their melancholy; for what we leave behind us is a part of ourselves; we must die to one life before we can enter another."

Learn to love yourself

What I've learned from spiritual teachings is that true respect comes from within, when we love ourselves. Not in a conceited or narcissistic way, but a healthy self-love. After all, if we don't love ourselves, how can we possibly feel the respect that others bestow on us?

We can be our own enemy and destructor of self-esteem. Therefore, we must silence that inner critic who spews negative thoughts about ourselves. One way to do this is by using affirmations, which are basically positive statements or self-talk. An example of this is Hay House Publishing founder Louise Hay's affirmation, "I love and respect myself." Such affirmations are known to be effective, but only if used as part of a comprehensive program of self-growth.

Simon, a young man who had just joined the Peace Corps when I interviewed him, shared this about his personal growth. He said he'd gained an amazing sense of peace and learned to enjoy the solitude of being alone. Most importantly, he had developed self-love, which had been his primary reason for going to Kazakhstan in the first place. He says he took some spiritual tools with him and used certain techniques, and that was all that was needed. He learned to be in the present moment, using mindfulness as a key element to access self-love. He believes it is "your number-one tool for dealing with any change."

An article on tinybuddha.com by Jenny Leigh called "Learning to Love Yourself: 3 Steps to Instantly Boost Your Self-Esteem" describes how Jenny found ways to increase her very low self-esteem. She recommends reminding yourself of the person you were by making a list of fifteen positive qualities about yourself. Then choose five and find examples of when you've been that way. For this step, however, she depends on the opinions of others, which may improve self-image but perhaps not intrinsic self-esteem.

The step that she says had the biggest impact on her self-esteem was when she kept a daily activity diary for achievements, fun, and relaxation. Practicing self-love and self-care improved her self-esteem: she says the steps she took helped adjust her negative core beliefs about herself.

Discover true self-esteem

Deepak Chopra explains in *The Ultimate Happiness Prescription* that "true self-esteem is not the same thing as improving your self-image. Self-image results from what others think of you. The true self lies beyond images. It can be found at a level of existence that is independent of the good and bad opinions of others." He adds, "When you shift your identity from your self-image to your true self, you will find happiness that none can take away from you."

Often when I've seen all my belongings in boxes, it's made me wonder if those possessions are who I am. On his "Awaken to Happiness" series on chopra.com, Deepak refers to this as "object referral, in which we identify with our self-image or external things, including our status, relationships, possessions, accomplishments, titles, and so on." He says object referral pulls us out of our true self and creates an "ego identity." The ego is insecure and motivated by approval and control. It can never find real peace and happiness, only a superficial level of existence. This can happen easily after relocating if a person feels insecure. Self-referral, the opposite of object referral, is where true happiness lies.

The following and final chapter of the book will talk more about how we can aspire to such a higher level of being and living. I hope it will help you feel at home within yourself and your environment.

In the End

What matters in the end
Is not how much I earned
How my career has grown
Or which cars or houses I own

What matters in the end
Is not whether I'm right or wrong
Whether I'm the ideal weight
Or that my teeth are white and straight

What matters in the end
Is how I lived my life
How many hearts I touched
And whether I'll be missed very much

That's all that matters in the end.

Kiran Prasad

Chapter 9

Higher Needs

One can choose to go back toward safety or forward toward growth.
Growth must be chosen again and again; fear must be overcome
again and again.

ABRAHAM MASLOW

At the top of Maslow's pyramid are cognitive, aesthetic, and self-actualization needs, generally known as higher-order or growth needs. In previous chapters, we discussed what Maslow called the basic, or deficiency, needs because he believed those must be satisfied before a person can aspire to the higher ones. However, people are unique and may not always follow this progression—it depends on their stage in life and their circumstances. For example, a young lady who moved from Italy to America with her husband told me she didn't miss family or friends at all. Obviously, she had less of a need for belonging than most.

Needing Beauty and Balance

Our higher order needs include the need for form, beauty, and balance in our surroundings. Aesthetic needs represent the desire for beauty, symmetry, and items that are artistically pleasing. We express our aesthetic sense by decorating our home, dressing fashionably, or even serving food in artistic ways.

My current home doesn't express my aesthetic sense because my husband chose it. In fact, I didn't even want to step inside it as a prospective buyer. Don't get me wrong, it's a great house with wonderful features and I'm truly grateful for it; it just doesn't reflect who I am as a person.

A 2011 *Telegraph* article by Leah Hyslop discussed a study by the Interchange Institute that involved over one hundred and thirty expats from twenty-four countries. The study, Hyslop reports, shows that choice of house, type of décor, and quality of neighborhood all make a huge difference to the moving experience.

As Susan Miller puts it in *After the Boxes are Unpacked*, where you live "is an extension of yourself, the essence of who you are. It reveals your identity." This is probably why it's hard to feel at home in a place that someone else has chosen or decorated.

This happened to Janika, the young lady who merged two families when she moved in with her boyfriend. Here's an interesting story she shared with me. I call it "The Elephant in the Room." Janika just couldn't relate to her boyfriend's place at first because the house was already a home, full of all his possessions. Therefore, she tried various ways to make it "homey" for herself, including putting up a shelf and placing her antique elephant on it. Janika admits it didn't even look aesthetically pleasing there, but when her boyfriend told her that and moved it somewhere else, she got extremely upset. She told me:

> I don't even know what it is about this elephant—it's an ugly wooden elephant. I guess it was just the fact that I wanted something of mine because I felt like there was nothing of mine in the living room. It was the principle

of it. And so I don't know why I had such a meltdown over this elephant. I just started bawling. I think it was everything. I guess we could just say "the elephant in the room," right? It signifies a lot. It's still a stupid elephant, but I'm not moving it and I don't care if he doesn't like it. I don't care if it looks ugly. The fact of the matter is it's *mine*.

Ivan, an architect friend of my children's, tells me that making a space your own is about putting your signature or mark on it, something "almost territorial," as Janika became over that elephant. Ivan remembers when he was at college and had to move to a room in his coed dormitory previously occupied by a girl named Samantha. He didn't do much to make it his own. In his first few months of living there, everyone kept calling it "Samantha's room" even though she was long gone. That bothered him because it was *his* room now. It didn't become his until about a year later, when he added a personal touch to it. He says that just with the addition of some paint, he could see the identity of the room begin to shift. "This is so me now," he remembers saying. "And the walls are covered with my architectural models and photographs. It's a psychological shift."

It starts with that fresh coat of paint. Choosing your own color for a space is the simplest way to make it your own and make it feel like home, Ivan says. He told me how Ray Eames, painter and wife of the famous architect Charles Eames, considered a house to be a blank canvas for people to fill. The Eames's house was filled with all sorts of knickknacks from their travels and was unmistakably their space. Ivan explained that the reason I still feel disconnected from my house is probably because it's "a fully painted canvas by someone else." I've made few modifications to it because it was already newly decorated and landscaped. This is something I'm not used to, as I've had to renovate all my previous houses extensively. With each small customization I make to my current house, it feels more like home.

Another, slightly more complicated, recommendation Ivan has for altering a room is through lighting. He explained how lighting is extremely transformative to a space. In addition to lighting, he recommends rearranging furniture to better suit your personal taste. He finds himself wanting to rearrange the furniture of others, and he helped both of my children make their college rooms aesthetically pleasing. He's a natural at it!

My friend Pamela possesses the same skill set: she was born to make spaces more pleasing for herself and others. Pamela tells me, "When I was eight years old, I designed my first home. It was for Malibu Barbie. It was made with record albums as walls, cardboard boxes for furniture, and Kleenex for bed linens." Once she outgrew Barbies, she says she regularly moved bedroom furniture around, much to her mother's dismay. Accessories would mysteriously switch around in her home. She even had the best-designed dorm room at college.

Now Pamela has her own design firm in California, Pamela Sandall Design. She loves her work, and feels that the process of "nesting" has always been her primary focus in life. She thinks it probably stems from changing homes every three or so years as a child. She explained that, after having a family of her own and nurturing them in the cozy environment she created, the desire to help others do the same shaped her career goals.

She told me about Avery, a client she'd worked with a number of years ago. Avery had bought furniture and decor from a catalog and wondered why her home still felt undecorated. According to Pamela, it didn't look undecorated; it looked exactly like the Pottery Barn catalog Avery had ordered from, but it didn't fit Avery and her family. Once Pamela personalized the room with carefully chosen décor and furniture to match their lifestyle, adding items that had been in hiding, Avery realized it had never been undecorated; it just hadn't felt like home.

Pamela's clients love that she first shops in their own home for beloved treasures. She stresses that we should relish our aesthetic surroundings. By using color, fabrics, design, family photos, travel treasures, memorabilia, favorite pieces of art, and favorite books, our home will nurture our family and us.

Not everyone can afford an interior decorator or buy new furniture. My daughter, who's just moved into her first rental apartment after college, has done a wonderful job of decorating it on her own. She used furniture and accessories that were given to her or that she acquired inexpensively. Whether you hire a designer or not, Pamela says that at the end of the day when you walk in, "Your house should greet you with a big hug."

Sometimes the landscape of a place can do quite the opposite, and repel us. Lisa, our frequent mover from England, said the landscape of Arizona was completely unfamiliar to her—nothing reminded her of home. She had no point of reference. Then, when they moved to Northern California and she saw a hedge, something she hadn't seen for a while, it really put her at ease. The landscape started to look aesthetically familiar and pleasing again. She thinks having just a few similarities stops you from feeling completely foreign. Having prior knowledge about the aesthetics of a place can also help.

Needing to Know and Find Meaning

Our higher-order needs include the need to know and understand, which represents our desire for knowledge, comprehension, and meaning.

Take educational classes

After relocating, we might find ourselves yearning to learn new things, or we may be required to for work reasons. Our cognitive needs depend on our circumstances and stage in life. If you're a first-time parent, you may want to pursue parenting classes. As an empty nester (veteran parent), it might be a further-education class. If you have the time and the opportunity, taking a class in something creative would be beneficial in easing relocation stress.

Make the most of the learning opportunities offered wherever you go. As a teacher by profession, I've always considered learning to be a lifelong endeavor that goes well beyond the realms of the classroom. This kind of real-life learning can bring great personal growth.

Gain spiritual knowledge and meaning

A transition such as moving can help us grow spiritually, too. When we're done searching through boxes of material possessions, we might find ourselves searching our souls for meaning. *Why am I here? What is my purpose?* Over the last few years, I've been immersing myself in the wisdom of the world's spiritual leaders. It's given my life meaning and helped me feel more connected to the world.

Develop a higher consciousness

One of the best pieces of spiritual knowledge I've gained that applies to moving is from Wayne Dyer, who passed away only a few days after my mother did. In a video, Dyer describes the three levels of consciousness with which we might connect with the world.

The first is Ego Consciousness, or when we identify with our ego. This is when we focus on outward things such as money, possessions, relationships, jobs, and titles. We also see others in those terms.

Another level is Group Consciousness. At this level, we identify people in terms of the groups they're affiliated with, or the differences between them such as skin color and culture.

In my "belonging" chapter I talk about how we're drawn to groups as a newcomer in order to fit in and be accepted for who we are. At the start of this book, I described how lonely and purposeless I felt. Now I see why: my ego or group consciousness probably contributed to those feelings of isolation. I saw people not as themselves, only as the categories I placed them into. I try to think differently now, but old habits die hard.

When we can see ourselves in others and understand that we're all one, we've ascended to Unity Consciousness. At this level, we're able to see past the artificial divisions we create and we no longer feel separate. It would be great if we could all aspire to this, but most of us are stuck at the previous levels of consciousness. Perhaps wars and the violence we see in our world these days could come to an end if everyone were at a higher level of consciousness. People functioning at this level are more likely to be self-actualized individuals.

Needing to Fulfill Our Purpose in Life

Self-actualization is at the peak of Maslow's pyramid, above all other needs, and is considered to be the ultimate goal. It's about being authentic, realizing our capabilities, and fulfilling our real purpose in life. Maslow believed that reaching our full potential is not a luxury but a real need, and that we should honor that calling.

A 2014 video on actualized.org called "Self-Actualization" by Leo Gura says most people just satisfy their lower-order needs and don't understand why they're unhappy. Self-actualization is what it means to be fully human. Lower-level needs keep you comfortable and secure, whereas meeting your higher needs allow you to live to your ideals, be passionate about life, really feel alive, and be your true self.

Self-actualized people are thought to have peak experiences, not unlike the experience of "flow" in our lives. One definition of "flow" is by Hungarian psychologist Mihaly Csikszentmihalyi, who describes it in a 2009 interview with *Wired* Magazine as "being completely involved in an activity for its own sake. The ego falls away. Time flies. Every action, movement, and thought follows inevitably from the previous one, like playing jazz. Your whole being is involved and you're using your skills to the utmost."

I never really knew what "flow" was until I started writing this book. I can truly say I've experienced it now: whenever I entered the world of my book, my mind became completely absorbed in the activity. Writing helped me get through difficult times by staying present and focused on my mission of helping others.

You might have another way of being "in the zone." We often say we're too busy to do the things we love best, especially when we're going through a transition in life, but that's when we most need to be present and aligned to our true self.

Qualities of self-actualized people

Leo Gura suggests that self-actualized people live in the present moment and are mindful in everyday situations. For example, they pursue higher values, are driven from the inside and not the outside, and strive for personal growth and improvement.

Personal transformation

In the last few years, I've experienced personal growth as I overcame various losses in my life. I was devastated, and I felt the kind of intense grief that I described at the start of the book. When I acknowledged these feelings and faced them head on, I was better able to go forward. What really helped was turning to self-help, positive psychology books, and other tools for personal transformation. These taught me to finally look at my losses as gifts or gains. I hope you're able to do that too.

Everyone or everything comes into our life for a reason: to teach us something. We have to be ready to accept that lesson. I know I wouldn't be writing and completing these last pages of my book if I hadn't gone through all the emotional pain and turmoil that loss brings. I'm grateful for it now because it has led to so much growth and transformation and has brought me to where I am today.

My life was on hold for too long, and now I'm finally emerging out of my cocoon. Wayne Dyer's *10 Secrets for Success and Inner Peace* helped me awaken to the fact that I have a really important purpose in life, and that I need to firmly set this as my intention and refuse to "die with my music still in me." Dyer's words and attending my mother's funeral made me realize how we can be gone tomorrow, and we owe it to the world and ourselves to share our gifts. It was what gave me the push I needed to complete this book and put it out there for the world. Like most writers, I could have easily lingered over it for many more years. Instead, I accepted that the time is *now*.

Use what happens to you

"The art of life is not controlling what happens to us . . . but using what happens to us," says Gloria Steinem in *Revolution from Within*. We can use our experiences of moving and other life transitions—even the loneliness and dark days—for a positive outcome.

Those with relocation backgrounds often become realtors, transition experts, relocation coaches, or authors. Why not use your experience to benefit others too? One place to do that is through Families in Global Transition (FIGT.org). This is an organization with an annual conference in which people from all backgrounds use their international experience to help other expats.

Reflection

As I reflect back to when I started writing this book and I could barely get out of bed in the morning because life had no meaning, I can see why I felt that way now. *I didn't know who I was.*

Like most of us, my sense of self was tied to the externals in life: a job, title, friends, relationships, a house that I loved, and possessions. These things can't provide lasting joy because they can all be taken away from us. I have since come to understand that I can be happy wherever I am because true bliss comes from within and nothing, or no one, can ever take that away.

I'm already at home. You can be too.

Namaste

References

Books

Bushong, Lois J. *Belonging Everywhere & Nowhere: Insights into Counseling the Globally Mobile.* Indianapolis, IN: Mango Tree Intercultural Services, 2013.

Bridges, William. *Transitions: Making Sense of Life's Changes,* 2nd ed. Boston, MA: Da Capo Press, 2004. First published 1980 by Addison-Wesley.

Bridges, William. *Managing Transitions: Making the Most of Change.* Reading, MA: Addison-Wesley, 1991.

Brown, Brené. *Daring Greatly: How the Courage to Be Vulnerable Transforms the Way We Live, Love, Parent, and Lead.* New York: Gotham Books, 2012.

Chapman, Gary. *The Five Love Languages: How to Express Heartfelt Commitment to Your Mate.* Chicago, IL: Northfield Publishing, 2004.

Chopra, Deepak. *Ageless Body, Timeless Mind: The Quantum Alternative to Growing Old.* New York: Harmony Books, 1993.

Chopra, Deepak. *The Ultimate Happiness Prescription: 7 Keys to Joy and Enlightenment.* New York: Harmony Books, 2009.

Colgrove, Melba, Harold H. Bloomfield, and Peter McWilliams. *How to Survive the Loss of a Love.* Los Angeles, CA: Prelude Press, 1991.

Deits, Bob. *Life after Loss: A Practical Guide to Renewing Your Life after Experiencing Major Loss.* 4th ed. Cambridge, MA: Da Capo/Lifelong, 2004.

Dyer, Wayne W. *Dr. Wayne Dyer's 10 Secrets for Success and Inner Peace.* Carlsbad, CA: Hay House, 2001.

Dyer, Wayne W. *You'll See It When You Believe It.* New York: W. Morrow, 1989.

Faber, Adele, and Elaine Mazlish. *How to Talk so Kids Will Listen & Listen so Kids Will Talk.* New York, NY: Avon Books, 1980.

Fast, Julius. *Body Language.* New York: MJF Books, 2002.

Frankl, Viktor, E. *Man's Search for Meaning.* MA: Beacon Press, 2006.

Geon, Bryan. *Newcomer's Handbook: For Moving to and Living in Portland.* Portland, OR: First Books, 2007.

Goleman, Daniel. *Emotional Intelligence.* New York: Bantam Books, 1996.

Harley, Willard F. *His Needs, Her Needs: Building an Affair-Proof Marriage.* 15th Anniversary ed. Grand Rapids, MI: Fleming H. Revell, 2001.

Hawkeye, Timber. *Buddhist Boot Camp.* New York: HarperOne, 2013.

Hay, Louise L. *You Can Heal Your Life.* Santa Monica, CA: Hay House, 1987.

Hay, Louise L., and David Kessler. *You Can Heal Your Heart: Finding Peace After a Breakup, Divorce, or Death.* Santa Monica, CA: Hay House, 2014.

Janssen, Linda A. *The Emotionally Resilient Expat: Engage, Adapt and Thrive Across Cultures.* London: Summertime Publishing, 2013.

Jarratt, Claudia J. *Helping Children Cope with Separation and Loss.* Harvard, MA: Harvard Common Press, 1994.

Johnson, Spencer. *Who Moved My Cheese? An Amazing Way to Deal with Change in Your Work and in Your Life.* New York: Putnam, 1998.

Levine, Leslie. *Will This Place Ever Feel Like Home? Simple Advice for Settling in After You Move.* Reprint, Chicago, IL: Contemporary Books, 2002.

Markham, Ursula. *Living with Change: Positive Techniques for Transforming Your Life.* Rockport, MA: Element, 1993.

Maslow, A.H. *Motivation and Personality.* 3rd ed. New York, NY: Harper & Row, 1987.

Miller, Susan. *After The Boxes Are Unpacked: Moving On After Moving In.* Colorado Springs, CO: Focus on the Family Publishing, 1995.

Morgenstern, Julie. *Organizing from the Inside Out.* New York: Henry Holt, 1998.

Muller, Wayne. *How Then, Shall We Live? Four Simple Questions that Reveal the Beauty and Meaning of Our Lives.* New York: Bantam Books, 1996.

Nansel, T. R., Overpeck, M., Pilla, R. S., Ruan, W. J., Simons-Morton, B., and Scheidt, P. Bullying behaviors among U.S. youth: Prevalence and association with psychosocial adjustment. *Journal of the American Medical Association*, 285, 1094-2100, 2001.

O'Donohue, John. *Eternal Echoes: Celtic Reflections on Our Yearning to Belong.* London: Bantam Press, 1999.

Parfitt, Jo. *A Moving Landscape.* London: Summertime Publishing, 2009.

Parfitt, Jo and Colleen Reichrath-Smith. *A Career in Your Suitcase: A Practical Guide to Creating Meaningful Work…Anywhere.* London: Summertime Publishing, 4th ed., 2013.

Pascoe, Robin. *A Moveable Marriage: Relocate Your Relationship Without Breaking It.* Vancouver, BC: Expatriate Press, 2003.

Pascoe, Robin. *Culture Shock! Successful Living Abroad: A Parent's Guide.* Singapore: Times Books International, 1993.

Pascoe, Robin. *Raising Global Nomads: Parenting Abroad In An On Demand World.* North Vancouver, BC: Expatriate Press, 2006.

Pellegrini, A. D. and Bartini, M. Dominance in early adolescent boys: Affiliative and aggressive dimensions and possible functions. *Merrill–Palmer Quarterly*, 47, 142–63, 2001.

Pollock, David. C and Ruth E. van Reken. *Third Culture Kids: Growing Up Among Worlds.* Boston: Nicholas Brealey Publishing, 2009.

Shield, Joseph. "Improve Your Life with Wayne Dyer's 3 Stages of Consciousness." YouTube video, 05:04. Posted January 2016. http://www.youtube.com/watch?v=CashRtgHl-0

Shimoff, Marci and Carol Kline. *Happy for No Reason: 7 Steps to Being Happy From the Inside Out.* New York: Free Press, 2008.

Steinem, Gloria. *Revolution from Within: A Book of Self-esteem.* Boston: Little, Brown and Company, 1992.

Stephens, Laura J. *An Inconvenient Posting: An Expat Wife's Memoir of Lost Identity.* London: Summertime Publishing, 2012.

Tinney, Rev. David, "Every Beginning Starts with an Ending" (sermon, First United Methodist Church of Vancouver, Vancouver, WA, April 13, 2008).

Thompson, Michael, Catherine O. Grace, and Lawrence J. Cohen. *Best Friends, Worst Enemies: Understanding the Social Lives of Children.* New York: Ballantine Books, 2001.

Tolle, Eckhart. *Stillness Speaks.* Novato, CA: New World Library, 2003.

Tolle, Eckhart. *The Power of Now: A Guide to Spiritual Enlightenment.* Novato, CA: New World Library, 1999.

Web Pages

Abbott, Maripat, 2014, "Present Moment Awareness in Relocation," *Manifesting Possibilities* (blog), http://holistic-relo.blogspot.com/2014/04/present-moment-awareness-in-relocation.html.

"Abraham Maslow," *The Pursuit of Happiness*, http://www.pursuit-of-happiness.org/history-of-happiness/abraham-maslow.

Ball, Aimee Lee, 2008, "Groundbreaking Research on Self-Esteem," *O Magazine*, http://www.oprah.com/omagazine/Groundbreaking-Research-on-Self-Esteem.

Baumeister, Roy F. and Mark R. Leary, "The Need to Belong: Desire for Interpersonal Attachments Is a Fundamental Human Motivation," *The American Psychological Association*, http://persweb.wabash.edu/facstaff/hortonr/articles%20f or%20class/baumeister%20and%201eary.pdf.

Better Health Channel, 2014, "Teenagers and Communication," https://www.betterhealth.vic.gov.au/health/healthyliving/t eenagers-and-communication.

Bosman, Julie, 2007, "When There's No Place Like Home," http://www.nytimes.com/2007/07/29/education/edlife/ homesick.html.

Bracken, Jeff, 2014, "The Important Difference Between Change and Transition," *Quality Texas Foundation*, http://quality-texas.org/wp-content/uploads/2014/11/The-Important-Difference-between-Change-and-Transition.pdf.

Civitelli, Janet S., Ph.D., 2015, "How to Survive Culture Shock When Moving for a New Job," *Vocation Village* (blog), http://www.vocationvillage.com/how-to-survive-culture-shock-when-moving-for-a-new-job.

Csikszentmihalyi, Mihaly, 2009, *Wired* Magazine (interview), https://www.wired.com/1996/09/czik.

Doland, Erin, "Scientists Find Physical Clutter Negatively Affects Your Ability to Focus, Process Information," *Unclutterer* (blog), https://unclutterer.com/2011/03/29/scientists-find-physical-clutter-negatively-affects-your-ability-to-focus-process-information.

Emrich, Michelle, "Abraham Maslow," Muskingum University, http://www.muskingum.edu/~psych/psycweb/history/m aslow.htm.

Fitzgerald, Megan, 2010, "Expat Expert Robin Pascoe Releases New Online Lecture Series on Successful Living Abroad," *Career by Choice* (blog), http://www.careerbychoiceblog.com/career_by_choice/20 10/09/expat-expert-robin-pascoe-releases-new-online-lecture-series-on-successful-living-abroad.html

Gilchrist, L.D., Schinke, S.P., Snow, W.H. et al., 1988, *Prevention and the Transitions of Adolescence*, Center for Adolescent Mental Health, Columbia University School of Social Work, http://www.ncbi.nlm.nih.gov/pubmed/24272164.

Gura, Leo,"Self Actualization,"
https://www.actualized.org/articles/self-actualization.

Hahn, Thich Nhat, 2006, "Returning Home,"
http://www.lionsroar.com/returning-home.

Hausman, Marcia S., and James R. Reed, "Psychological Issues in
Relocation: Response to Change," *Journal of Career Develop-
ment*, 17, no. 4 (June 1991): 247–258,
http://link.springer.com/article/10.1007%2FBF01359142.

Ho, Derek, 2010, "Homesickness Isn't Really About Home,"
CNN,
http://www.cnn.com/2010/HEALTH/08/16/homesickn
ess.not.about.home.

Huitt, W, 2007, "Maslow's Hierarchy of Needs," *Educational Psychology Interactive*,
http://www.edpsycinteractive.org/topics/conation/maslo
w.html.

Hyslop, Leah, 2011, "Unhappy Expat? It's Time to Change Your
House," *Telegraph*,
http://www.telegraph.co.uk/expat/expatnews/8319160/U
nhappy-expat-Its-time-to-change-your-house.html.

India Parenting Pvt. Ltd.,"Hindu House Warming Ceremony (Griha Pravesh)," *India Parenting*,
http://www.indiaparenting.com/home-and-
decor/59_828/hindu-house-warming-ceremonygriha-
pravesh.html.

Kershaw, Sarah, 2010, "The Psychology of Moving," *The New York
Times*,
http://www.nytimes.com/2010/02/28/realestate/28cov.ht
ml.

Leigh, Jenny, "Learning to Love Yourself: 3 Steps to Instantly
Boost Your Self-Esteem," http://tinybuddha.com/blog/3-
steps-instantly-boost-self-esteem/

Pascoe, Robin, "Culture Shock in the Digital World,"
http://www.figt.org/Resources/Documents/new%20reso
urce%20center/culture_shock_in_the_digital_world.pdf

Phipps, Nikki, "Blended Families: Merging Two Families Under One Roof," *FamilyLobby.com*, http://articles.familylobby.com/434-blended-families3a-merging-two-families-under.htm.

Reynolds, A.J., C.C. Chen and J.E. Herbers, 2009, "School Mobility and Educational Success: A Research Synthesis and Evidence on Prevention," *University of Minnesota*, https://iom.nationalacademies.org/~/media/Files/Activity%20Files/Children/ChildMobility/Reynolds%20Chen%20and%20Herbers.pdf.

Sam I Am, June 22, 2007 (post to forum), "Relocation Depression: I Give Up," *City-Data.com*, http://www.city-data.com/forum/mental-health/101267-relocation-depression-i-give-up.html.

Solera, Connie, *Dirty Footprints Studio* (blog), http://www.dirtyfootprints-studio.com/blog.

The Chopra Center, "Week 3: Discover Authentic Self-Esteem," http://www.chopra.com/online-programs/8-week-happiness-series/week-3-discover-authentic-self-esteem.

Thoits, Peggy A., and Hewitt Lyndi N. "Volunteer Work and Well-Being." *Journal of Health and Social Behavior* 42, no. 2 (2001): 115-31. http://www.jstor.org/stable/3090173.

Thurber, Christopher A. and Edward Walton, 2007, "Preventing and Treating Homesickness," *AAP Gateway*, http://pediatrics.aappublications.org/content/119/1/192.

Useful Links

ChopraCenterMeditation.com

> *Meditation series by Deepak Chopra and Oprah Winfrey.*

ExpatriateConnection.com

> *A resource for expats, especially accompanying spouses.*

FIGT.org

> *Connection and resources for the globally mobile.*

IWasAnExpatWife.com

> *An expat wife shares about expat life.*

Meetup.com

> *The world's largest network of localized interest groups.*

NAMI.org

> *Mental health support from The National Alliance on Mental Illness.*

NewcomersClub.com

> *Listing of international clubs for newcomers.*

NewcomersHandbooks.com

> *Guides for moving to and living in popular U.S. cities.*

Psych.community

> *Support community for depression sufferers.*

SunBox.com

> *An online retailer selling light-therapy boxes.*

StopBullying.gov

> *Information from various government agencies on what bullying is and how you can respond to it.*

SusanMiller.org

> *Christian guidance for dealing with relocation grief.*

Made in the USA
Middletown, DE
14 October 2017